The Unlimited Freelancer

The Unlimited Freelancer

Published in Media, PA, by FreelanceFolder.com
Edited by Natalie M Miller and Andrea Sullivan

ISBN: 978-0-578-02252-9

This book is dedicated to all who believe in entrepreneurship and the power to fight for one's own destiny.

Contents

Systems, Software, and Automation (cont.)

Building a Freelance Team

Revenue-Generating Assets

Combine Strategies for Unlimited Potential

Section One

How to Be an Unlimited Freelancer

Overcome freelance limits and Unleash your full business potential

Introduction

Would you like a life that lets you grow, enjoy more free time, do what you love every day, make more money, and build a valuable business?

If you said yes, then this book is for you. Optimizing your freelancing business can be a big part of reaching your dreams and goals of more time, more money, and more freedom – and that's what being an Unlimited Freelancer is all about.

The Unlimited Freelancer is written for freelancers by freelancers who have been right where you are – flying solo, flying scared, flying whole-heartedly towards our dreams and goals. Each of us has built a successful, sustainable business for a better life. To us, freelancing is about the freedom to chase and achieve the life you want.

The internet opened the doors for freelancers worldwide. The low start-up costs allow just about anyone to jump into freelancing. People with all sorts of skills and talents are freelancing their way these days.

Freelancing isn't all bright and sunny, though. Many freelancers quickly find themselves in difficult situations:

- Being overworked and underpaid
- Scrambling to meet deadlines
- Constantly needing to find more clients

- Wishing for free time, weekends, and vacations
- Frustrated by too much administrative overhead

Freelancing is tough. It can be *very* difficult, in fact. It can wear people down, making them lose sight of what they used to love because they have to do everything else just to get by.

The problem is that freelancing often ends up being a job you've built for yourself, and it's no more freeing than any other job out there. You can't get tired, you can't get sick, and you certainly can't get bored or your income will suffer – you often have less vacation than ever before. Sometimes freelancing feels like a prison sentence.

This situation is common. Many people enter into freelancing without knowing the obstacles they'll face. They're unprepared, and they really don't know what they are getting into.

Freelancing doesn't have to be frightening, scary, or tough. There are ways to leverage tools and resources to overcome obstacles, grow your business, and do what you love. With a little knowledge, you can easily get around the common challenges.

That's not all, though. With the right information you can completely remove your limitations as a freelancer – and open your business to enormous amounts of potential. You could go from a solo freelancer to a multi-person, multi-million dollar company.

All you need is to change your mindset. Freelancing isn't your job; it's a business. Your business should be working for you to help you reach your goals. It should have systems and processes that make your life easier. It should make money even when you aren't around.

Of course, you need to learn exactly how to do all of that, which is where this book comes in.

This book will show you ways to change your freelancing job into a thriving business, one that you can grow or refine as much as you want.

You'll learn how to:

- Leverage resources to free up more time
- Use systems to reduce your overall workload
- Outsource boring tasks and do the work you love
- Boost income with partnerships and collaboration
- Create assets that generate recurring revenue
- Put it together to create a self-sustaining business
- Remove your barriers, increase your potential

... and start doing what you love to do.

Who We Are

We're regular people just like you. There's nothing magical or special about us at all. We're just a pair of freelancers, solo entrepreneurs, and small business owners who have applied everything we outline in this book to build our own successful freelance businesses.

Our businesses, SmallFuel Marketing and Men with Pens, are healthy, thriving, and providing many people with a decent living. They make us a lot of money, and the blogs we maintain are read daily by thousands of people, bringing valuable tips and advice to web workers of the world.

Our businesses aren't important to us because they're popular, though. Our businesses are important because they let us pursue other projects, provide us with continual income, and create jobs for other people, too.

They allow us to work less, make more money, and enjoy the freedom of freelancing.

Life wasn't always that good, though...

Where It All Began

We began our businesses the same way most freelancers did: tired of working for someone else, we saw the potential to earn money doing what we loved, and we jumped right in.

It was a tough road – we learned about running a business the hard way. We each knew a ton about how to deal with customers, the operations of a business, ways to manage projects and ultimately how to deliver satisfaction, but we knew nothing about working for ourselves.

So, we made the same mistakes other freelancers make all the time. We worked long hours, invested all our energy into doing everything, and never took a break. We felt guilty we didn't spend enough time with our families, and all we did was work.

We both quickly realized that our businesses were running us, and not the other way around.

At the Mercy of Business

When we started freelancing, we were slaves to the business.

If the business required a worker, we did the work. If the business needed a bookkeeper, we crunched all of the numbers. If the business needed a customer service rep, we took the phone call. If the business needed a marketing director, a manager, or an associate – we were the person for the job. We did everything.

Each time our business needed this, that, or the other, we were the only person it could turn to for help. We'd boxed ourselves into being the single employee that filled too many positions.

The worst part was that there wasn't enough time in the day to earn the income we wanted. We were working flat out and money was still tight; every hour we weren't working on client projects cost us money.

What about that life of freelancing freedom? Well, it just wasn't happening. Our businesses were controlling us.

So we quit our jobs – and started building businesses.

There's a Better Life Out There

A freelance business should work for its owner, not the other way around. It should support a lifestyle, provide income, and let the owner work on what he or she enjoys.

A freelance business should run on its own steam, giving the owner more free time, more money, and more freedom to expand or pursue other ambitions.

If you don't want to expand into a big company, building a freelance business will offer you greater earning potential and a lot more flexibility. If you do want to expand, then this information is even more important – you'll need it to attain serious growth.

The techniques we explain in this book are some of the best ways to achieve freelancing success. We cover all of the important elements of growing your business and making it work for you. We also show you how to build a business with the potential for massive growth and expansion, should you want to do that.

By implementing the right business systems, building a distributed team, and creating valuable assets, there is almost no limit to what you can achieve. You really will be an Unlimited Freelancer.

It's also important to note that this book was a collaborative project and a joint-venture partnership. Its very existence demonstrates how any freelancer can work with other people to boost business potential.

It is a great example of our business methodology in practice.

About This Book

We want people working on their own to learn how to have a better life, one that lets them do what they love and love what they do – each and every day.

That's why we wrote this guide, to provide freelancers with strategies and techniques to turn a limiting freelance job into a healthy freelance business.

Each chapter will give you valuable lessons and resources for working less, earning more, and growing a healthy, thriving business.

Good luck, enjoy your read, and we wish you the best,

– Mason and James

How to Be An Unlimited Freelancer

Building a business that allows you to overcome the usual limits of freelancing isn't as complicated as you might think. We can show you most of what you need to know right in this book, and then all that's left is to implement these ideas for yourself.

In this chapter, we'll be going over the theory of becoming an Unlimited Freelancer. We'll talk about the typical problems of freelancing, the difference between a freelance job and a freelance business, and then about how you can overcome those problems to unleash your full potential. Let's begin with a story.

Charles had been operating his graphic design business for nearly a year now. What had first been an exciting adventure in freelancing was now becoming a serious problem.

He didn't want to get up in the mornings. All the work he faced was overwhelming. He was tired of answering emails and had stopped returning client calls. A project with an upcoming deadline wasn't finished yet, and the pressure and guilt were really starting to get to him.

Charles found that every time he sat down to work, he couldn't seem to get as much done as he wanted. There was always something cropping up that he needed to take care of. He'd tried some productivity and time management tricks, but they didn't really do anything. They just seemed to add to the work!

One evening before bed, Charles turned off his computer. He'd put in 14 hours that day, and he still hadn't finished everything that needed to be done. He just didn't care. He realized he didn't like his freelance job anymore.

The next week, Charles applied to work in the office of a local company. He landed a dull office job, and it would be three years before Charles took up designing again.

The Difficulties of Freelancing

Without question, freelancing is one of best ways to earn a living. Despite all of the benefits, though, there are a lot of difficulties that go along with it. Working at home, on your own, without an office or staff poses several unique problems – that sometimes make freelance life seem like a nightmare.

Here are some of the most common challenges:

The Feast or Famine Cycle

Freelancers have only a limited amount of time and are naturally trying to earn as much as possible. The result of this time crunch is that freelancers are forced to decide between spending time marketing and spending time working on client projects. This typically causes the number of active client projects to fluctuate between far too few and far too many.

Maintaining a Work/Life Balance

Despite our workload and challenges, no freelancer works in a vacuum. We all have families, friends, hobbies, and other parts of our lives where we need to spend time. Balancing the amount of time spent on work and the amount of time spent on other areas of life can be really difficult.

Managing Everything by Yourself

The amount of information and tasks that are required to manage a business is enormous, and the amount of time required to run it all is no less so. Freelancers are required to deal with everything from accounting, to marketing, to client projects, and more. To take care of everything, freelancers must use a significant amount of time from already low reserves, and still there are often issues that go unhandled.

Dealing with Emergencies

No freelancer is immune to sickness, nor are any of us capable of completely isolating ourselves from family or other emergencies. Emergencies are a normal part of life, but for freelancers they can be even more difficult because there's rarely anyone else can take over the business. When there's no one running the business, income and everything else suffers – often making the situation even worse.

Fighting Negative Perceptions

There are all sorts of negative perceptions towards freelancers, both personal and professional. Professionally, freelancers are often thought of as less serious or less skilled than a larger business, and this can lead to fewer contracts that are worth less money. On the personal side, it's often difficult to get away from the perception of having lots of free time or being able to go out during the middle of the day.

The good news is that all of these freelance challenges have a universal solution – and that is to start looking at your freelancing like a business, and not a job.

Building a Job or a Business

Freelancers give up on their businesses for many different reasons, but one of the most common (and correctable) causes is that they end up building themselves a job, not a business. Often times they come to hate that new job as much as the one they just left.

People quit their jobs and build new jobs for themselves all the time. They didn't enjoy what they were doing, so they decide to print up some business cards, open a business, and become self-employed. As a freelancer, they have many more opportunities and can become their own boss.

In many cases, though, freelancers are just exchanging one type of employer for another – their clients. These new customers have needs to be fulfilled, and there's only one employee available. Every time the business has a need, someone has to answer. Sound familiar?

Success in freelancing depends on a wide number of variables and factors – but it primarily depends on ***you***. There is only so much of ***you*** to go around, and that's why it's important to build a business that can work for you, and not a job that constantly takes your time and energy.

Take Away:

Many freelancers fail because they create businesses and then go to work for their businesses as employees. A business should work for the owner – not the other way around.

How to Build a Thriving Business

The good news is that creating a thriving freelance business isn't as difficult as you might think. There are three main parts to liberating yourself from the typical freelance challenges and preparing for significant growth.

Systems and Automation

A good business uses a collection of software and systems to automate as much of the predictable work as possible. These systems should take care of many tasks entirely on their own and should make much of the other work significantly easier for you. In this way, the business is leveraging your time so that in one hour you can actually complete the equivalent of, say, 4-5 hours of work.

Working with Other People

As a freelancer, you might think that you have to do everything on your own – but that simply isn't true. Using other people in your business can help leverage your time even further and make it possible for you to take on more clients or offer more services than ever before. Many times, typically through partnerships, you will be exposed to opportunities you wouldn't have if you were to remain entirely on your own.

Products and Assets

A revenue-generating asset is something that you can create once, and earn profit from for a long time. If you've heard of passive income, a revenue-generating asset is much the same thing. These assets typically take the form of a product or business that you can earn money from on a regular basis – typically without an enormous amount of work. It could be a software package, a book (like this one), a website, or any number of other things. These assets increase the stability of your income, and they also offer the opportunity for enormous growth.

Making the most of your time is the crucial factor to building a great business. After that comes making the most of your money and making the most money in the least amount of time. When all of these factors are properly balanced, you'll have a business that makes enough money for you to be comfortable, leaves free time to grow the business, and has the potential to grow into anything you want.

This ideal business will make the greatest use of everything you put into it – both time and money. Everything you do will be leveraged to have significant and profound results, and you won't need to spend any of your valuable time working on things that aren't of real importance to the business.

Once you get to this point, your goals and dreams will easily be within your grasp.

The Benefits of a Business

As we mentioned before, there are clear benefits to becoming a business owner. A freelance business provides a vast array of solutions to the common solo freelancer problems, lowering the risk of failure and increasing your opportunities for success.

Now we know you're eager to get to the part about building your business, but before we do it's good for your motivation to see what you're working for. Here are some of the benefits you'll get by becoming a freelance business owner:

More Free Time

When you collaborate with others, use business systems to automate tasks, and outsource monotonous work, you reduce the amount of time you spend doing tasks you don't like. These tasks hold you back, so get rid of them.

Delegation and automation allow you to free your time so you can concentrate on projects you enjoy. You could implement business improvements, explore passive income streams, work on strategies to gain clients… or just take some well-deserved time off.

Higher Customer Satisfaction

By leveraging the skills and talents of other people and integrating applications into your business, you have the opportunity to offer clients better services, more services and higher quality work.

When clients are more satisfied with your services and receive more of what they desire, they'll keep coming back to your business. Their higher rate of satisfaction earns you happy customers willing to refer more people to your business, so it's win-win all around.

Improved Services

When freelancers make the switch from being the sole worker in a business to an owner who knows how to leverage resources and streamline operations, the result is often a marked improvement in services across a wide range of areas.

Less stress and a more balanced workload offers better results for your clients. It's easier to make good decisions when you're rested and have the time to think carefully.

Working with other skilled people can bolster your weaknesses and improve the quality of your work. You'll probably even be able to deliver work faster.

Learn From Others

Working and collaborating with other people gives you the potential to learn new skills from someone with more experience or different skill sets than your own.

This increased knowledge can be a great advantage and benefit for your business, not to mention your own personal success. You might discover a hidden talent, be able to

> "This year we've already launched four sites, with another half-dozen penciled in to go up before 2009. Some of those are more in our marketplace and TUTS lines, but we also have a couple of brand new ideas to launch too. It's a pretty exciting time for our little company which started out in my living room not so long ago. These days we're still mostly working in living rooms, just more of them!"
>
> *Collis Ta'eed, FreelanceSwitch and Envato*

command higher rates, or expand your current services to include new ones that you can now offer.

Greater Earnings Potential

A freelance business has better money-earning potential than a freelance job. Solo freelancers face limitations and restricted capacity, but businesses have no limits or restrictions at all.

Businesses can also do more for clients than anything a single person can do. Businesses produce faster, handle larger projects, have better access to skilled workers, and maintain a steady stream of production over a longer period of time.

The only limits in business are the ones that you choose to set for yourself – based on your goals and desires.

Do the Work You Love

Delegation, collaboration, and automation allow you to focus on the work you love the most and the work that you do best. The result is that you'll feel a higher level of personal satisfaction and fulfillment.

You might end up falling in love with your work all over again. Not only that, since you're more excited about the work you produce, you'll usually do a better job.

Work Less

A business will allow you to leverage your time so you get more things done with less work. Getting more out of your day means you can create a business that takes on a great deal of work, while you end up doing much less than you were before.

In short, by expanding your business to include other people and the right systems, you will work smarter, you'll work less, and you'll get a lot more done. Some business owners barely even work at all, and their businesses operate smoothly without them.

Accept Better Projects

There's nothing more disappointing than turning down the perfect project because of an overloaded schedule.

If you have a well-set business, you don't have to say no to great projects. You no longer have limitations on what you can accept. You can collaborate with people who enjoy all types of work, and you can keep the best projects for yourself.

You also won't worry as much about a lack of work, as you'll have the time to market continuously and build up a bigger customer base.

Create Investments

Building a business into a profitable, thriving venture with a good reputation and a solid client base is a smart way to create an investment for your future. A profitable business will not only earn a lot of money, but it is also worth an enormous amount money if you chose to sell it.

Many investors buy successful businesses. If you want the money, or even if you just want to do something else, you could always sell your business for a significant profit.

Provide Financial Security

Freelancers often forget possibilities like falling sick, becoming injured, or having health issues later in life (sometimes sooner than expected). While no one likes to think about the loss of a limb, losing an eye, or spending life in a wheelchair, these events could occur.

Insurance helps, but policies may not pay out enough – or may not pay at all, depending on the situation. Also, proper insurance coverage is expensive in the first place.

Owning a business that is somewhat autonomous can provide you with income even in the event of an emergency.

Create an Exit Strategy

Solo freelancers can rarely step away from their business without it crashing. If you're the sole employee of a business that needs your support to operate, who will fill your shoes if you need a break?

A freelance business that operates more independently will also provide a better exit strategy for you. With other people able to fill the roles you previously had to fill on your own, you can take a vacation, retire, pursue other projects, or move on to create a new business while this one continues to provide revenue for you.

Build a Legacy

If you're a parent, you may want to build a nest egg for the future. Maybe you want to provide a means to pay for your child's education, or leave something for your children when you pass on. A freelance business is an asset that can help.

A business is part of an estate that your children can inherit. Your children could sell the business for financial security. Or, if your children choose to do so, they can work in the business alongside you, learning how it operates so they can continue maintaining it and enjoy the revenue long after you're gone. Your business could provide a legacy for generations to come.

Take-Away Message:

Businesses offer many benefits, allowing for more free time, increased revenues, and better exit strategies. A good business gives its owner a solid income base and peace of mind.

Let's Begin

Now that you've read through this first section, you should have a good grasp on the benefits of creating a business versus simply working in the job of freelancer. You should also have an understanding of how the solo freelancer mindset can hold you back from reaching your goals and dreams.

In the next section we get into the details of how you can apply some of this to your own business, specifically software, systems, and automation.

We cover techniques for automating the tasks and actions you do regularly: everything from client interactions, to marketing, to project fulfillment, to administrative duties. You'll learn which areas of your business are the best to systematize, and how to find software or create workflows to handle those areas. We then go through several of the most common systems and provide examples and resources that you can use in your business. It's time to get into the meat of running a successful business.

Section Two

Systems, Software, and Automation

How to streamline your business and super-charge your efficiency

Using Systems

Systems are a key part of making your business efficient, consistent, and easy to run. By using systems alongside the proper software, you can streamline many of the tasks that you do on a regular basis – saving time, saving money, and giving you the opportunity to grow your business further.

Before we get into the subject, though, it's important to know what we mean by 'systems'. Here's our working definition:

> *A system is a set of rules, a workflow, or a procedure that takes a repetitive task and moves it through a specific set of steps towards a predictable result.*

While that might seem complicated at first, it's actually pretty straightforward. You probably already have some sort of a system in place. In fact, it's quite likely that you do.

Your daily routine is a type of system, for example. You wake up, have coffee, check your email, and look over the day's jobs. You get to work, and at the end of the day you have results.

That's a system.

Of course, your daily routine probably varies a lot, so it doesn't make for the best type of system. The best systems are used for activities that don't change a lot – like managing a particular type of project or sending an email blast to your customer.

Think of a system like a production line in a factory. The raw goods (your task) move through the machines (the steps to completion) and at the end of the conveyor belt, out comes the finished product (the result).

> "Waste is a constraint. Reducing waste in your organization is one of the easiest ways of reducing constraints."
>
> *Michael Port, Author of Book Yourself Solid*

Setting up systems for your business helps you:

- Create predictable results
- Automate repetitive tasks
- Complete work quickly
- Increase efficiency
- Improve collaboration
- Increase quality of work
- Increase response time

In short, systems save time and money while increasing customer satisfaction, production speed, and often the quality of your work.

Systems also reduce and eliminate the wasted energy that goes into repetitive tasks. By clarifying the exact steps required to perform an activity, it's easy to cut out unnecessary work and distill the process down to its core.

You can apply systems to almost every aspect of your business. Some of the systems will need to be specific to your line of work, but there are other areas that tend to work well for systems no matter what your business.

The Best Areas to Systematize

"What a mess." Carolyn complained to her friend. "I'm so busy now, I just can't seem to find anything. I feel like I'm taking care of everything as it comes up, and it's not working."

Carolyn's business growth had caused disorganization. She hadn't had a system in place for managing client contacts and maintaining follow-up communication. Now she felt scattered, disorganized, and confused.

So one day she sat down and created a checklist. She wrote down everything she had to do when she submitted a proposal. She made sure that the process didn't double up anywhere along the way, and that the steps followed each other logically.

The next time Carolyn had a proposal to write, she whipped out her checklist and ran through it. It saved her 15 minutes.

The next day, she had two proposals to submit. She used her checklist method and saved 30 minutes. Four days later, she saved another 15 minutes.

By the end of the month, Carolyn had 'found' 8 hours that she hadn't had the month before – and she realized she felt much better about the proposal submission process. "I run through proposals like a machine!" she laughed.

When developing systems for your business, the goal is to eliminate and reduce all unnecessary work and to make the core process as efficient as possible. It's about finding the best method to get the job done, and then using that method over and over.

For an activity like writing a proposal, a system is a perfect fit. In our story above, Carolyn used a simple checklist to make her proposal writing faster.

What if you were to take it one step further, and create a template for your most common proposals? How much time could you save? It's these types of thoughts that will lead you to building efficient systems in your business.

Finding Systems in Your Business

Here's a process to see what systems might work for you:

Step 1 – List

Sit down somewhere quiet with a pencil and paper, and write down every business activity you do on a regular basis – think of as many as you can. What daily tasks do you have? How about weekly? What work do you do for clients? How about administrative work?

Step 2 – Organize

Look back at your list of tasks, and start crossing things off. Cross of anything that you love to do; cross off anything that needs complete customization. When you're left with the annoying tasks that take up a lot of your time, see if you can combine them into related groups.

Step 3 – Plan

You should be left with a few groups of tasks that you do regularly, like sending and following up with proposals. Now, consider what parts of these are repetitive, and how you might be able to do the work once and reuse it in the future. Put that into an outline – or find a piece of software to help – and you've just created a system.

When you're finished working through these steps, you'll see that there are a lot of different places where you could use systems. Some of the systems would be rather complicated, like accounting or project management, while other areas would be a lot simpler, like creating a process for managing customer contact information.

Completely systematizing a business can be an enormous task; there are many areas of your business that will require you to design a workflow and system from the ground up for your exact process. The good thing about systems, though, is that you can implement them slowly and streamline your business over time.

You don't need to get bogged down right away in creating brand new systems for your business – you can focus on implementing the many pre-made systems and applications already out there.

Most businesses share at least the basic operating procedures, and people have been creating systems for those areas for decades. By working with these existing systems and software applications you can reap the substantial benefits of automation with very little work and time.

The easiest and most common areas of systemization include:

- Accounting, Billing, and Bookkeeping
- Customer Relationship Management
- Project Management and Collaboration
- Marketing, Promotion, and Publicity

In each of these areas of your business, you can easily apply or tailor existing systems, implement existing software applications, and use pre-made strategies to reduce your workload.

Even without building a completely custom system, there are many ways you can integrate existing systems for your own needs. Try different combinations, explore various methods, and test out several applications to see which serve your purposes best.

It's a good idea to start work on the areas of your business that can immediately be improved by integrating applications. There are hundreds of great applications, almost one for every need, and you'll be able to make substantial progress before even needing to get into custom solutions.

In the following sections, we take a look at some of the best applications, strategies, and tricks for each of the common areas we listed previously. We've based our suggestions on our own experience and research, and the experiences of freelance business we've worked with. Remember, what works best for some people may not be what works best for you.

What matters is that you discover ways to start optimizing your business so you can see just how to turn it into a streamlined success.

Automating Your Accounting

Far too many freelancers don't properly maintain their books, probably because it's so frustrating to do. Many freelancers can't stand numbers at all. They don't understand bookkeeping, aren't familiar with the terms, and consider maintaining clean books a serious headache.

Even the smallest of small freelance businesses needs to have properly maintained books for future financial success. If you really want to grow, it's even more important. One mistake can come back to haunt you years later, and it could potentially require hours of expert help to unravel a financial mess.

Money is the lifeblood that keeps your business alive, and accounting is what keeps it organized. This is the area where you can see if you're making money, know when you're losing it, examine where money is being spent, etc...

If you're going to pay attention to any area, accounting would be the first.

Our strongest recommendation is that you buy accounting software or use a web-based accounting system that helps you avoid having to calculate anything at all. These systems, like QuickBooks and IAC-EZ, let you quickly and easily enter basic data, and they provide you with all sorts of reports that either help you monitor your business financials yourself or allow you to print reports out and bring them to your accountant.

Another good reason to automate bookkeeping is that you can hand over your bookkeeping to someone else so that you don't have to take care of it. IAC-EZ.com, for example, is so simple to use that anyone can enter the data without having any skills at all. Collect all the receipts and hand them over to your bookkeeper or a Virtual Assistant to enter the information. If you want to enter data yourself, that's fine too.

Some freelancers use online invoicing systems like FreshBooks or Zoho Invoices, but remember that these systems aren't enough to cover all your accounting needs. There is much more to bookkeeping than invoicing and collecting. You need to monitor business expenses, like printer ink and membership fees, and you'll need to see if you're earning a profit or coming up short.

Invoicing systems, though, can help you reduce additional bookkeeping tasks, and they work nicely in conjunction with accounting software to heighten accuracy and speed up processes as well. Let's look at a quick example.

Situation A: No Accounting or Billing System

Jordan just got a new client project and can't wait to get home to start the process. As soon as he's back, he fires up Microsoft Word and creates a quick invoice. When he's done with the invoice, he sends it over to his new customer.

His new customer receives the invoice and sends a check back over to Jordan, who then deposits it at the bank and sends a receipt to his customer (which he created manually in Word).

After sending the receipt, Jordan opens up Microsoft Excel and enters the payment and customer name to keep for his records. He'll use this to calculate taxes later on.

Finally, long after the project is complete, Jordan opens up all of his Excel records and manually calculates the information he needs for his taxes. He puts all of that together and sends it to his accountant.

The previous example is a common situation for many responsible freelancers. Jordan was even using some basic systems, but overall there is a lot of wasted time. Let's take a look at someone using a more ideal setup.

Situation B: Accounting and Billing System

Cara just got a new client project and can't wait to get home to start the process. As soon as she's back, she fires up Freshbooks and enters the project costs and the client's contact information.

Freshbooks automatically emails an invoice to the client and provides several payment options. When Cara's client sends payment, the system automatically sends a thank you email with a receipt. Freshbooks also provides a website where the client can view their past invoices, payments, and receipts.

The invoicing system synchronizes regularly with Cara's online bookkeeping software, IAC-EZ, so at the end of the year she only has to push a button and all of her information will be formatted and ready for her accountant.

This second example shows how much time you can save by implementing a few easy systems. The example software we mentioned in Cara's system is only one possible combination out of thousands. Depending on your clients and your methods, you can choose something that works best for you.

Accounting Resources and Software

There are a ton of great applications for invoicing, accounting and bookkeeping to help you get started, but here are a few top picks that have been recommended by many freelancers:

QuickBooks http://www.quickbooks.com
This system does it all, and very well. If you deal with multiple currencies, they have a version built just for that. There's also an online version for web-based use.

IAC-EZ http://www.iac-ez.com
This system is fully web-based and turns bookkeeping into a breeze. Data entry couldn't be any simpler. At the end of the year, just click a button to get a certified professional to do your tax reports.

Less Accounting http://www.lessaccounting.com
This is another web-based system that makes accounting significantly easier for freelancers. They also interact with many of the other online systems.

FreshBooks http://www.freshbooks.com
An invoicing system used by many freelancers, FreshBooks has a great reputation and always ends up being a very popular choice. They have a free version as well as a premium version.

Zoho Invoice http://invoice.zoho.com
Low-priced, high-quality web applications are Zoho's specialty. Their invoicing system lets you manage estimates, invoices, and payments. It's also great for freelancers working with multiple currencies.

Other Systems and Applications to Try:

Complete Accounting Systems:

http://www.gobootstrap.com
http://www.xero.com

Invoicing or Billing Systems:

http://www.billingmanager.intuit.com/billing/welcome.url
http://www.simplyinvoices.com
http://www.invoiceplace.com/invoice/
http://www.blinksale.com/home
http://www.invotrak.com
http://www.invoicesmadeeasy.com
http://www.billmyclients.com
http://www.billingorchard.com
http://www.simplybill.com
http://www.time59.com
http://www.bill4time.com
http://www.paysimple.com
http://www.getcashboard.com

http://www.invoice2go.com
http://www.getharvest.com
http://www.trac.edgewall.org
http://www.clickablebliss.com/billable
http://www.bambooinvoice.org
http://www.curdbee.com

Your Financial Backbone

Because proper accounting is so important to the financial health of your business (and its ultimate survival), determining a good system that works for your business is crucial.

Bookkeeping is the backbone of your whole business, the skeleton that affects the body of your business, so it's one area you should never neglect.

There are no reasons to avoid proper bookkeeping anymore, either, considering the great applications, software, and tools that put all the power into your hands, even if you have no training at all. Bookkeeping has become so well automated and simple that you no longer have to become a numbers whiz.

Why bother? Can't you hire someone for that?

There are a few fantastic reasons to stay on top of your accounting and understand exactly how the system works, even if you hire others for assistance (which you should).

First, the more information you have about the financial health of your business, the better. You can make smarter decisions and keep better track of what is and is not working.

Two, you'll be aware of problems that arise and be in a better position to find a solution. You can plan ahead and budget for slow seasons, and you can monitor the various financial indicators of your business.

Three, you'll be 100% prepared if you need discuss your financial documents with banks, investors, or the government – and this happens more often than you might think.

Avoid Accounting Headaches in the First Place

Accounting is often an area that makes a freelancer's head spin, but there are easy ways to maintain your books in the least amount of time – and with the least amount of frustration, too.

1. Get the right software. Don't skimp in this area, and make sure that the accounting software you choose gives you exactly what you need.

2. Set up a good payment processing system. Choose a system that works with your accounting software, such as PayPal for QuickBooks, and add in the applications that make extra tasks a breeze, like FreshBooks.

3. Get the training you need. Buy a book on basic accounting, take a course online or locally, or hire a bookkeeper to teach you daily maintenance tasks.

4. Set aside time to learn the proper ways to enter data, bill clients, collect money, and record transactions.

5. Set aside a specific time every day, every couple of days or once a week to maintain your books and record transactions. Never neglect your books longer than one week, unless you want to end up wasting time and struggling.

Take Away:

Accounting is one area of business many freelancers set up poorly and neglect. It's also one of the easiest areas to deal with and automate, making it a good area to focus on improving.

Spend time setting up the right system and tools, invest in yourself to get a bit of training, and develop the proper maintenance schedule to make this aspect of your business a success.

Managing Projects Using Systems

Project management is one of the best areas that you can systematize. Chances are you won't be able to automate everything, since the bulk of the work will probably require your attention, but you can save a lot of time by creating a framework that organizes and streamlines the work you do.

With a good project management system in place, many areas of your business will start to come together. The efficiency with which you handle projects directly relates to how many of those projects you can take on at one time – which impacts your growth potential. A good system can significantly increase that potential.

Growing your business to new levels requires a lot of work to be handled concurrently, and a good framework for handling that work is key. Whether it is client projects or internal projects, you need to be able to organize and complete your work as efficiently as possible. That's what a project management system is about.

Benefits of a Project Management System

Managing projects properly is important to your business. The more you know exactly what's going on and when it will happen, the better you can serve your clients to keep them coming back for more. Here are a few of the benefits to using a system for this:

- **Work faster and more efficiently.**
  Whether you're managing a project on your own or managing a project involving many people, the right system cuts down on the time you have to spend working. Applications help centralize related discussions, files, and task lists in one place so that everything is easy to find and never gets lost. They also help organize and direct your work effort, so you get results faster and don't waste any time.

- **Improve transparency and collaboration.**
  Everyone involved in the project can see what others are doing, if you choose to let them view the information. That means Fred knows what John is doing and when he can expect John to send him the files to work on the next step. Or it means that customers can watch their project in real-time without having to email you every hour for updates.

- **Streamline and enhance communication**.
  Most systems will automatically email collaborators when new information becomes available, and the entire team can discuss together rather than depend on you to pass on their notes. You can even allow clients

direct access to their projects and let them provide feedback during progress.

- **Improve Accountability.**
  There's less room for mistakes or missed deadlines, and everyone's work effort can be seen by all (should you wish). Collaborators become directly responsible for their deadlines, which takes some weight off your shoulders. If you're working alone, a schedule and calendar will still help you meet deadlines.

- **Monitor progress and capacity.**
  Even if it's just your own progress, by monitoring completed tasks, milestones, and deadlines, you'll be able to keep better track of what's going on. This helps you schedule and manage your time more effectively so that you eliminate that scattered feeling. You'll be 100% informed on what's going on in your business at all times. You'll know what projects are in the works, when you'll have space for new clients, and when you can expect to collect client payments. If you stay on top of your business, you're definitely on your way to success.

- **Easily delegate work**
  You can easily assign someone on your team to the project management position, letting them supervise the project and work with collaborators. That lets you work on your own projects or rest easy; and when you need to check in, all the information you need is just a click away.

Choosing a Project System

There are many project management systems you can use, from free to premium and from web-based to something you can download. Be careful that the system you choose doesn't include too many bells and whistles that clutter up your process, but also be sure to choose a system that provides as much of what you need as possible.

You can find expanded management systems that let you centralize even more information and depending on your business, this might be valuable. Enterprise resource planning systems, for example, include not only project management, but also sales, accounting, leads, and more.

If possible, it's a better idea to find an application that answers many needs instead of just one. If you can find a single application that does five different things for your business, it's probably better than using five different applications for each area of your business. On the other hand, finding an all-in-one system that works well for your exact processes can be very difficult. The best way to see if that will work for you is to explore a variety of applications to get a feel for what's available.

Ultimately, the best choice is going to be the one that you enjoy working with, that works best in your business, and that saves as much of your time as possible.

Recommended Applications

Of the hundreds of great project management and collaboration applications out there, we've compiled a list of applications that we recommend most:

Active Collab http://www.activecollab.com
This system has a beautiful interface and tons of features like checklists, tickets, file sharing, discussion areas, and more. It comes in two versions, both of which you buy once and own forever.

Basecamp http://www.basecamphq.com
A popular choice, Basecamp is a web-based hosted project manager with discussion features, file sharing, milestone tracking and more. There are multiple pricing options to fit your business needs, all of which are monthly subscriptions.

WORKetc http://www.worketc.com
This little jewel is a project management system that also lets you enter orders, invoice clients and take care of some bookkeeping tasks. If it has the features you need, it could be a great all-in-one system.

Zoho Projects http://www.projects.zoho.com/jsp/home.jps
Zoho offers a suite of web-based applications that help business owners manage projects and much more. If you have a large variety of needs, it might be a good idea to look at the many systems they offer.

Other Systems and Applications to Try:

http://www.drop.io
http://www.attask.com
http://project2manage.com
http://www.comindwork.com
http://www.liquidplanner.com
http://www.aceproject.com
http://www.goplan.info
http://www.projectplace.com
http://www.projectdesk.net
http://www.sosius.com
http://www.jointcontract.com
http://groupswim.com
http://www.propel-it.com
http://www.dotproject.net
http://www.5pmweb.com
http://www.jexxe.com
http://www.centraldesktop.com
http://www.interprisesuite.com
http://docs.google.com

A Look at Your Project Framework

Here are a few tips for using getting started with a project management system:

1. Choose the right application. Web-based is usually the best choice because it allows collaborators (and yourself) a way to log in from any location and stay updated on any projects.

2. More is better. When you're looking for an application, sample as many types of software as you can. Find something that gives you the features and tools that are most effective in your business.

3. Get a set of instructions in place before you begin to use your software; from 'how to communicate' to 'how to follow up on your tasks'. Write down these instructions, and make sure to send them to anyone else using the system. You need to be clear in telling collaborators what they are responsible for in the system.

4. See number three. Do not skip this step or downplay its importance. The clearer you can make guidelines for everyone working on a project, including yourself, the easier, faster and better projects become.

5. Be firm. Most people resist using unfamiliar applications. They may try to stick to old methods and habits. It's up to you to enforce (gently, mind you) that this project management system is part of how you do business.

6. Be ready to accept feedback and suggestions. There are always better ways of working. Ask people if they see new ways to use the application.

7. Take the time to familiarize yourself with the application. Do not skip this step. It's tempting to dive right in, but the tutorials, instructions, help wikis, etc. for the application often provide tips for even faster usage to make projects progress super-smoothly.

8. Get into the habit of a daily progress check. Log in, view each open project, and make sure they're exactly where they should be. Ask for updates and stay on top of what's happening.

Getting started with a project management may seem like a lot to handle, but once you get the system running it is entirely worthwhile.

Project management takes some time to get used to, so stick with it! Develop a habit, explore the application you decide on, and use it for all it's worth. The rewards are fantastic, the time you'll save managing your projects will be greatly reduced, and within a few weeks you'll wonder how you ever managed before.

Take-away Message:

Project management is the basis for being able to handle more work in less time. A good project management system will significantly improve your organizational abilities, your collaboration potential, and the overall capability of your company to complete projects.

When implementing your system, explore many applications to find one that best fits your business model. Look specifically at collaboration, good management tools, and other automation features. Once you implement a project management system you'll never look back.

Contact and Relationship Systems

As a freelancer, there are countless people that you need to communicate with on a regular basis. In a freelance business, there are even more people to keep track of. Organizing all of this information and keeping on top of these interactions is very important for building a business with maximum potential.

Communication is an essential element of all areas of a business, and in many cases it can mean the difference between success and failure. Clients appreciate good communication, vendors provide better work with better instructions, and other business relationships and partnerships will be much more plentiful if you are good at maintaining your contact.

The size and value of your personal network is directly proportional to how well you are able to communicate and manage these communications. There are several key areas where you can systematize your communications.

Systematize Your Communications

There are many applications available to help you organize contact information, communication, sales information and more. These applications range from the simplest database for storing phone numbers and email addresses, to complex customer relations management systems (or CRMs) that allow you to monitor and track leads through to fulfilment.

These applications are fantastic for saving time and staying organized. For example, client management applications let you store phone numbers, email, and other contact information for all of your clients so you always have it handy. You can also keep track of every vendor or business contact you come across, too.

Each of these applications accomplishes two major goals:

1) Centralizing all of your important information in a single location.

2) Automating as much of the contact process as possible, and helping you handle the rest.

A good customer management application offers some interesting features for the freelance business. For example, ZohoCRM lets you see a client's past orders, the frequency, and the amount the client ordered. You can monitor all your clients and orders, taking note of patterns, strong sellers, and the overview of sales.

CRMs can help you track leads, too, so that can turn leads into clients. With email, it's easy to forget to follow up with potential customers, but a CRM system will make sure you are in touch with the right people at the right times.

Many CRMs also have task or activity flows, where you can create a list of follow-up actions and run through that list with every new lead you enter into the database. Most simpler CRMs still let you add tasks so you can keep track of what you need to do and when. In many cases, just a quick follow-up can turn a lead into a customer.

CRM Systems and Applications

Finding the right contact management system will take a little bit of searching. The size of your venture often has little bearing on the type of system you'll want, and there are many varieties to choose from.

Depending on the types of contacts you communicate with, and what your contact processes look like, you may want a CRM system with many or few options. Feature-rich CRMs tend to be harder to use at first, but offer greater flexibility in the long run. Smaller and slimmer CRM systems tend to be very easy to use, but may not have all of the options you desire.

Here are a few of the favorite systems among freelance business owners:

Zoho CRM http://crm.zoho.com
This system is feature-rich, yet still relatively easy to use. It even integrates some additional features like vendor and invoice management, so the result is a complete customer management system. Best of all, it's free for less than three users and very inexpensive after that.

SalesForce http://www.salesforce.com
This is the CRM system for people who have their sights set on maximum flexibility and maximum features. SalesForce is an industry favorite among small to medium size businesses and can grow with your company no matter how big you are.

Sugar CRM http://www.sugarcrm.com
Sugar CRM offers a nice interface and some great features for customer management, and it's open source, too. Its "Sugar Exchange" offers add-ons and plug-ins as well.

Highrise http://www.highrisehq.com
Made by the people who created the popular Basecamp, Highrise is great for tracking leads and keeping contact information handy.

Other Good Systems and Applications to Try:

http://bigcontacts.com
http://www.salesboom.com
http://www.rightnow.com
http://www.salesjunction.com
http://www.genius.com/us/products/salesgenius.html
http://www.stazzle.org

http://www.consideredsales.com
http://www.freecrm.com
http://www.relationals.com
http://www.appstacks.com

Your Communication Framework

Communicating with customers, potential customers, businesses, vendors, and others can take a significant amount of time. Using some of these recommended CRM systems, you can reduce the amount of time that is required to keep in contact with a given person.

The goal is not to reduce the customer care you provide or to contact fewer people, but to actually improve your service and maintain contact with as many people as possible – all the while spending less time doing it.

The more you automate and systematize tasks within the area of customer relations, the more efficiently you can handle any customer request that comes along; from initial contact to troubleshooting. This helps you provide great service, which is a key quality for small businesses today.

By managing your contacts efficiently, you can work less to bring consumers into your business as clients, and those clients will be much more satisfied with your service. It's a win-win situation all around.

Here are some ways you can start working less and improving your customer relations.

Create Templates

Over time, you'll notice that many customers have similar requests. You'll find yourself repeating words you've already said to many different people and answering a lot of the same routine questions too.

You can reduce the amount of time you spend answering those routine questions by creating templates for the common answers. This can significantly impact your speed of service and immediately improve your efficiency.

Template replies are great for questions that have standard answers; such as your payment and business terms, or an outline of your service process. When composing emails, simply copy and paste the section of the text you need and shave more minutes off your day. If you write your template well, you may only need to switch out the client's name.

Use Your Website as a Communication Platform

Your website can serve as a communication hub for your business – providing information, answering common questions, and even getting the right information from new customers.

For example, you can customize your website with contact forms that clients can fill in if they're looking for services. You could have a contact form with fields for the type of work clients seek, their budget for the project, their preferred method of communication, or the turnaround time they desire. You'll reduce the amount of time you spend

> "Not only can systems help to encourage better use of your time, but they can also lead to a better product or service. You probably have a lot of experience in your field and you've learned some things over the years that help you to know what produces the best results. Systematically putting these things into practice can lead into a consistently high quality of work."
>
> *Steven Snell, VandelayDesign and DesignM.ag*

going back and forth to discover this information and you'll be better equipped to respond to potential customers rapidly.
Another great way to use your website is to create questionnaires for routine questions you need answered before beginning a new project. If you're a designer, for example, you can ask questions about branding, preferred colors, target market and more. If you're a writer, you can ask about word counts, preferred tone, and style of language.

Choose Your Client Contact, and Set Limits

The easier you make it for potential clients to get in touch with you, the better – but it's important to know which methods cost more time than they bring in money, and it's just as important to know which methods work best for you.

For example, many businesses offer phone and email communication to their clients. What if you hate talking on the phone? What about using instant messaging instead? What if you don't type well?

Why not use Skype and schedule calls? Too many freelancers feel forced into communicating in ways they don't enjoy.

Find the ways that work best for you, not just for clients. Post clear information on your site about when clients can contact you. You're a businessperson – you don't need to accept calls at the crack of dawn if you don't want to.

Always make sure that you use time efficiently. If you're going to call a client, know what you'll discuss beforehand, what answers you need and how long you want the call to take. The same goes for instant messaging. Your time is just as valuable as a client's, so use it wisely.

Clean Up Your Email

How you organize and manage your email can have a huge impact on saving time. Many freelancers use the default mail settings and don't customize their filtering. For example, the inbox becomes one giant "catch-all" that has every type of email you receive, from all different places.

Use your email to its fullest potential. Categorize and organize so that when you look back through past communications (and you will), you're not faced with sifting through hundreds of emails or racking your brains for the best search terms.

No matter which email system you use – Outlook, Gmail, or Thunderbird – folders and labels will work to keep email nice and neat.

Here's an example of what you can do with email filtering:

1. Split customer communication into three categories: Potential, Active and Inactive.

2. Label each new communication you receive with one of the three category names.

3. Label each new communication further with the customer name.

Your email labels or folders would then look like this:

Customer Communication \ Potential \ Sally NoName

When a potential customer becomes active or when an active customer becomes inactive, re-label or move the client's folder to the appropriate category. Go ahead and categorize further if you'd like; grouping emails by type under the client umbrella.

The above example is just one of many ways you can organize your email. Whether or not that specific example works for you, you should have *some* sort of email organization. It will significantly lower the time it takes to maintain communications.

Take-away Message:

Examine the various business communications you have, and find the ones that you do on a regular basis. Create a workflow or process for those contacts, and find a CRM system that will make things easier.

Then, further improve your communications by using templates to answer frequently asked questions, using your website as a communication platform, and creating a structured and organized email system.

Marketing Automation and Systems

Believe it or not, there is a substantial amount of marketing that you can automate completely. That's right – once you have the system set up you could be getting new clients with barely any effort all.

There are various systems that allow you to accomplish this, most of which are online or web-based. The internet is a fantastic platform that can easily serve as your central marketing hub.

Even if your customers are offline, though, there are still some ways that you can automate your marketing. For example, there are several websites that allow you to create a postcard campaign that is sent automatically to the addresses of your customers, on a timed basis.

Marketing Your Business Online

Marketing isn't always about passing out business cards or buying ads in local newspapers. Much of your marketing can be automated so that you act once and reap rewards over the long term.

Your web presence is the first place to start. The power of a proper website, with a good design and compelling copy, is unbelievable. It's also one of the cheapest, easiest ways to market your business these days.

In fact, your web presence can become your 24/7 salesperson, working for you day and night while you sleep, eat and play. If you don't have a website, then you have to do all the work of convincing people you're right for the job. If you do have a website, it can do all of that for you, and any expenses you incur pay for themselves repeatedly.

The best part is that virtual presence is a marketing strategy where you put in the effort upfront and reap the rewards for years to come. Your site starts working for you by attracting customers with a nice-looking and well-branded design. Your content can then help convince people that you're the best choice for their needs.

You can put up an FAQ on your site and post answers to common questions, saving you the trouble of always responding personally. You can integrate a payment system, making buying from you a breeze. You can implement forms, surveys and questionnaires so that you don't have to spend time asking.

Even if you have a one-page profile with a simple list of your services and contact information, you'll still increase the number of people who do business with you when compared to having no website at all.

Why stop there, though?

You can spruce up your contact form to capture key information from potential customers, such as their budget or type of project. Go beyond just having the client write what they want – prompt customers with questions you need answered right away.

Integrate other neat forms into your site as well. For example, Wufoo.com lets you build forms so that you can have people who buy your eBook or template design answer a few questions after payment. That helps you serve future customers better. Alternatively, you can poll new visitors to your site and find out exactly what they're looking for so that you can respond to demand.

Your imagination is the only limit on what you can automate with your online marketing. If you need something, chances are good that you can find a plug-in, a module, or a coder that can make it happen for you.

Imagine an automated process where potential customers land on your site, decide to hire you, and can fill in questionnaires right on the spot. They can even pay for your services, submit information and receive confirmation – all automatically. Their order comes in, and you can set up the production, confirm the delivery date, and get right to work all while barely touching anything.

It almost sounds like a dream, but it most definitely isn't. With some upfront effort and a little work on a regular basis, your website can leverage your marketing efforts so everything that you do is multiplied by hundreds or thousands of visitors.

Does web presence require great skills? Not anymore. Many applications and programs help you achieve a professional site without knowing much about technology. And if you do get stuck, there are plenty of businesses skilled in website design and setup that are ready to help you out.

Automating Your Marketing with Email

Marketing with email is one of the best ways to grow your freelance business. An email list will keep all of your biggest fans just a single click away, and you can use automated emails to bring new readers or leads into the fold.

There are several different ways to use email to help automate your marketing process. One of the most recommended is to use an auto-responder to help take somewhat interested website visitors and turn them into extremely interested potential customers.

By putting some useful information into an email series of 5-7 messages, you automatically start marketing to new subscribers as they are added to your list. They'll receive your messages in order and quickly become closer to your business.

Another way to use email is by offering a free download or other incentive to sign up for a list. You can then send email-blasts to the entire list when you have promotions or other information you want to spread. Email systems like AWeber and ConstantContact make this relatively easy to do.

Marketing via Social Media

Social media marketing is a topic worthy of an entire book on its own, but it deserves at least a mention in this chapter. Social media is a powerful way to gain new customers, and you can automate your participation somewhat.

It's important to be very careful when automating social media, though, because it's very easy to go too far and remove the 'social' part, which will greatly reduce the effectiveness of your efforts.

The best way to streamline social media is to find systems that leverage your time – so you can continue to maintain the social aspect, but you spend less time doing so.

An example of this is using social media aggregators – systems that collect information from multiple social sites in one place. These aggregators allow you to input your updates once and have them distributed to various networks, and they can substantially reduce the effort it takes to see results.

A Complete Marketing Strategy

Marketing is a key element of taking a freelance business and preparing it for maximum growth. Planning to increase capacity will do little if you don't have the ability to fill that extra capacity with new clients, so it's important to create that demand and be able to find more work once you can handle it.

If you are already operating at capacity, a good marketing strategy will serve as a way to ensure you have your choice of a variety of clients to work with, and it will provide insurance in case of a dry spell in work.

Take a look at the following marketing strategy, and think about how you might apply it to your business. Here's the overview:

1. **Lead Generation and Promotion**
2. **Trust and Relationship Building**
3. **Prospect Follow-Up System**
4. **Closing the Sale**
5. **Long-Term Prospect Engagement**
6. **Customer Experience Program**
7. **Customer Marketing and Referral Program**

Let's take a look at each one of these steps in a little more detail.

1. **Lead Generation and Promotion**

   No matter what type of business you're marketing, lead generation is always the first place to start. We recommend networking online, writing useful content, guest posting, and even offline marketing as some of the most effective ways to find new leads.

   You'll want to maximize your profile and build awareness by getting your brand in as many places as possible. By building your business profile, you will naturally start to get more leads.

2. **Trust and Relationship Building**

   The most important part of getting new customers is building the trust and credibility necessary to have people buy from you. Before someone will commit their hard-earned money to your services, they have to know that you will have their interests at heart.

   You can increase trust by offering something of value for free (advice or information), by showing previous work you've completed, and by getting great testimonials and referrals. Also, the simple act of communicating with someone over a period of time is a good way of increasing trust.

   Once your prospects trust you enough, it is only a matter of maintaining the relationship until they are ready to become a client.

3. **Prospect Follow-Up System**
   Rarely will anyone remember a business they see after only a single encounter. It is easy for you to fall out of their field of view and eventually be forgotten in the shuffle. For this reason, it is important to make sure your name and business are periodically put in front of them.

   As soon as a potential customer is found, you should quickly contact them by either emailing, calling, or meeting in person. If they don't want to talk, or don't contact you back, follow up again within a month or two to see if the situation has changed.

   The key to this step is proving that you are a reliable and long-term company. It will also ensure that, when the time is right, potential buyers will think of your business.

4. **Sale Closing Method**
   When the previous stages of this strategy are implemented, closing the sale becomes relatively easy. Your prospects should already know and trust you, and now it's simply a matter of pointing out how you can save them money or help them get work done. Once you find the right fit, it should be an instant sale.

5. **Long-Term Prospect Engagement**
   Many of your prospects won't be in the position to buy right away, even if they really want to. For best results, it's important to you keep your business in

front of them and hold them close to your company while they wait for the right time. These long-term prospects are the ones that aren't really ready to buy (so you won't be personally following-up with them) but are still viable leads for the future.

One of the best ways to keep your long-term prospects around is by setting up a blog, email newsletter, or some other sort of regular informational broadcast. Sending this out on a regular basis will keep your followers close and often times, bring in many new ones.

6. **Customer Experience Program**
   Once you complete a sale and turn a prospect into a customer, the marketing is just beginning. It's crucial for you to manage customer expectations and create a program that guarantees they will be impressed with your company and satisfied with your services.

   A few recommendations include: maintaining regular contact throughout all projects, assigning realistic timelines and periodically beating them, and occasionally sending unexpected gifts (cards, articles, anything). Happy customers will be your best source of new business.

7. **Customer Marketing and Referral Program**
   While keeping your customers happy is usually good enough, we also recommend creating a marketing program specifically targeted at your current customers.

The focus of the customer marketing program should be to generate repeat business from existing clients, and to encourage them to refer new clients to you.

A few ways to implement this include: a customer-only newsletter with special deals and incentives, a periodic mailing, referral bonuses, and other similar ideas.

A Few More Marketing Tips

Many strategies help you market your business without having to invest much time or energy. You can automate some of your tactics, streamline others, and build on the results. Your efforts will soon pay off, drawing in new customers without having to seek them out.

Here are a few more tips that might be helpful:

Business Means Business Cards

Many freelancers don't feel that they can use traditional business marketing tools to help themselves earn more clients. For example, many don't have business cards to hand out. That's a mistake.

Business cards are very cheap marketing tools, and all you need to do is have some made and pass them out. Leave them in conspicuous places where people will notice and potentially pick some up.

Post Your Rates

Post your rates to your website to spare yourself the task of answering, "What do you offer?" and "How much will this cost?" You eliminate window shoppers and tire-kickers: two types of potential customers who waste time and rarely become clients.

If you want to keep your rates and service offerings private, that's fine too. Have the descriptions of what you offer and the rate you charge written out in a template response so that you can cut and paste the information into emails.

Package your Deals

Create packages for your products or services to standardize what you offer to clients, save time, and create better income potential. Packages save time in production. You'll know exactly what goes into each package, making the process predictable enough to streamline even further.

In addition, you also save time because you'll no longer have to create individual, personalized quotes for each client.

Advertise

Advertising is another way of marketing your business without working too hard. One small ad placed in a good location can get noticed by thousands of people, each one a potential customer.

It's important to have a good ad, of course; a visually appealing one that has a short, catchy message. We recommend having a professionally-designed ad that you use on many different sites to maximize exposure and reach more people.

Make sure you analyze the results of your advertising. You need to know which ads and placements brought the most returns to your business. For example, an ad seen by 1,000 people that only result in 10 customers isn't as effective as an ad seen by 100 people that results in 5.

Analyze your Efforts

Imagine you advertised on a forum, ran a guest post at a blog, and launched a special promotion – all at the same time. How would you know which marketing strategy was the most effective?

You can analyze many of your marketing efforts via website tools like Google Analytics, which lets you know which people landed on your website, what they read, how long they stayed, and where they clicked while they were there. Site analytics can tell you a lot about your target market and the strategies that are working for you.

Take-away Message:

Marketing is a critical system for any growing freelance business. Operating near your maximum capacity is always the goal, and a proper marketing strategy will help achieve that.

Much of your marketing can be automated, and anything that is done over the internet is an exceptionally good candidate. Remember that in some areas your marketing system is there to increase the amount of human connections you make, and not to replace them altogether.

Marketing Resources and Applications

With technology growing in leaps and bounds, there's no way we can list all the options out there to help you get your business online and market it effectively.

But we can certainly help you get started with our tried-and-tested top picks:

WordPress - http://wordpress.org
Known primarily as being a blog platform, WordPress has grown quickly into much more than that. It is one of the best website platforms in existence today. You can create a simple profile site, have a website/blog combo, or create a complete online gateway for your business.

ExpressionEngine http://expressionengine.com
This website platform provides an extremely flexible system that can be used for nearly any web ideas you might have. From blogs, to stores, to forums, ExpressionEngine can do it all.

Wufoo http://www.wufoo.com
This is one of the neatest little form builders we've ever seen. You can create questionnaires, after-purchase surveys, new client captures, and more, and you can easily place the forms directly into your website.

Aweber http://www.aweber.com
One of the best email marketing systems around, AWeber is easy for even the novice email marketer to use, and it

offers many features that will unleash your marketing potential.

Google Analytics http://www.google.com/analytics
Sign up for this, copy some code to your site, and start monitoring how people found your website, what they did while they were there and which areas of your site are the most popular. This is one of the best ways to see which of your marketing efforts are really paying off.

Other Good Systems and Applications to Try:

http://www.emailwave.com
http://www.constantcontact.com
http://www.icontact.com
http://www.verticalresponse.com
http://www.mailchimp.com
http://www.joomla.org
http://www.drupal.com
http://www.movabletype.org
http://www.twitter.com
http://www.friendfeed.com

Implementing Systems When You're Too Busy

Janice was all for improving her business. She had bought books to teach her better processes, she had downloaded eBook guides that were going to increase her productivity; she had even signed up for a course on business management.

She never made it to the course.

Not only did Janice miss the course, but she also never read the eBooks she'd downloaded. She hadn't even picked up the books she'd bought, and they were still sitting on a shelf, waiting to be read.

It wasn't that she didn't want to spend the time learning better ways to freelance. She just didn't have the time.

Janice was already overworked. There was a lot to do in a week, and finding the hours she needed to sit down and finally read those books was impossible.

If Janice spent an hour reading, it would be an hour less that she worked. It would be an hour's income, too. And it was an hour that she'd have to make up somewhere else. She was tired enough as it was.

"One day," Janice told herself. Right now, she didn't have time to spend learning systems and better business management. She had work to do.

Creating a systems-based set of processes isn't easy. We'll admit it. It's going to take some work. Building a better business does take time, thought, and effort on your part.

But the payoffs are well worth it. Investing your energy enables you to you create increased revenue, less work, and smoother operations in the future. The sooner you begin developing your systems, the better.

It's a great idea to start building when your business is small and you don't have many projects or tasks filling your day. That way, when you begin to get more client work, you'll be set to accept and manage the growth more easily.

But what if your business has already grown?

What if you're already overloaded and can't even catch two minutes to breathe? How can you create a system when you're strapped for time?

Unfortunately, there are very few options. You're going to have to pull back a bit and find the time. This may mean temporarily taking on less work or fewer clients and sacrificing some current income.

Keep in mind that the situation is temporary. The period of cutting back to make more time isn't permanent, and you will shortly be back in the full swing of production – with more time for yourself and the beginnings of a solid support base for growth.

Find the time you need and the focus required so that you can build the proper foundation to unleash your full potential. Your business deserves it, and you're worth it.

One Step Back, Two Steps Forward

The first step to take if you're already overwhelmed with work is to decide just how much sacrifice you can afford to make. Big chunks of time are good – often people need to devote a full month towards improving their business, because it gives them the necessary time to focus and a chance to concentrate on what they need to do.

If setting aside a month of time and losing that income doesn't sound feasible to you right now, that's okay. You may just have too much work to finish up or need money too badly.

Figure out how much time you *can* afford to set aside so that you can work on your business. Promise yourself one day a week to work on your business – or even an hour a day. You'll be tightening your belt, but remember, it's temporary.

> "The biggest advantage to developing and using systems in your work is the potential for improved efficiency and productivity. We all have limited time available to work, and as freelancers that directly impacts how much money we make."
>
> *Steven Snell, VandelayDesign and DesignM.ag*

Once you decide the amount of time you can commit, give yourself definitive restrictions – and stick to them. You may have a hard time holding yourself to your own personal commitments at first. A project that pays well may be tempting, or a favorite client may really need you right now, but remember that you will have many more of these opportunities after you've systematized your business.

Give time to yourself. Clients won't hate you forever if you say, "Thank you, but I'll have to pass this time." Customers won't be upset and turn away for life if you say, "I'm booked solid next week, but I'm free the week after."

You could even partner with a trusted peer for the time that you'll be busy and refer clients to that person while you work on your business.

You need to take care of yourself and your business. Your future matters. Cheating yourself on this opportunity only puts you back where you were – spending too much time working in your business. So be tough with yourself. Stand firm, and know that you're giving yourself a gift.

Remember: Your crazy work cycle will never stop until you find a way out of it. Say "yes" to yourself and your business and start making it happen.

Snowball Your Way to More Time

One trick to jump-start the process is to use the snowball effect to claw back time.
Start by picking a small task that you know in your heart someone else can do. Maybe your email needs some organization, or you could benefit from email templates to use when responding to clients. Organized email and template replies save time – time you could can use elsewhere.

Outsource the tasks to a Virtual Assistant (also known as a VA). Then pat yourself on the back, because you've just gained a few minutes in your day. You're on your way to getting your time back.

Now pick another small, easy task you usually perform. How about light bookkeeping? Anyone can do that. Your brain isn't the only one that can do data entry in Excel or Quickbooks. Try outsourcing that too.

Billing and invoicing is another easy area to outsource – very easy in fact. Ask a VA to invoice a client when their project is complete, and let the VA handle the invoice creation, emailing and collection.

Guess what? As you shed yourself of extra work by using the snowball effect, you'll find that you have increasingly more time to work on setting up streamlined systems and processes for your business. And even better? Those systems will free up even more time.

Take-away message:

Freelancers often have so much work to do that they don't have the time to improve their situation. By cutting back on work to increase free time, many freelancers can spare enough time to start streamlining and implementing systems.

For those who are too busy, or can't afford to cut back, outsourcing certain tasks can be a good way to get back small chunks of time – with which you can begin implementing systems.

Section Three

Building A Freelance Team

How to outsource, partner, and work with other people to create a scalable team

Why You Need a Team

As a freelancer, you're probably used to being hired by other companies, not being the one doing the hiring. For you to think about hiring another person might seem a little strange at first, but that's exactly what you need to start doing.

Most of the big freelance limitations are a direct result of the limited time and output of a single person. There is only one of you, and there are only so many things you can do in a workweek.

By working with other people, you can begin to leverage the time you have to get more results. You'll be able to accomplish significantly more work in the same amount of time.

Teams Create Leverage

Let's look at this idea of *leverage*. Here's a diagram of a typical client project without using leverage:

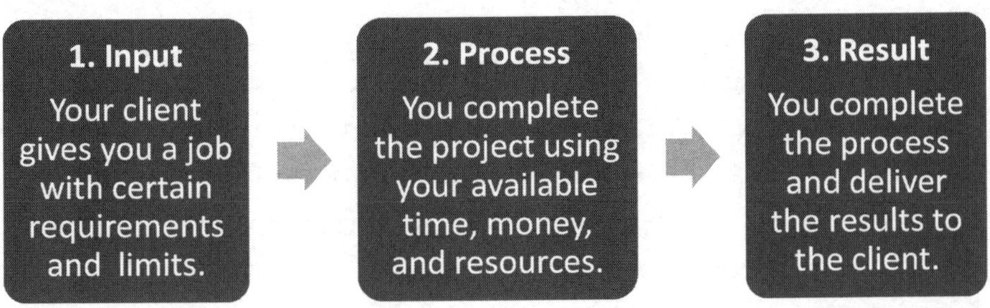

In this scenario, your time and completed work have a 1:1 ratio. Every hour of your work creates one hour of results – and your business can only earn as much money as the work you can do. There is essentially a salary cap on your company based on how much time you can spend working.

Let's look at the same process using a leveraged system.

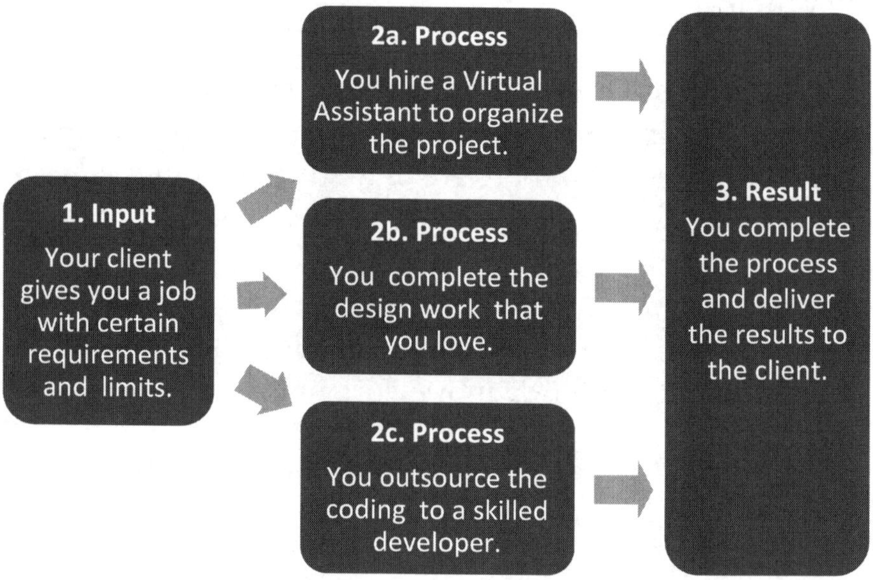

In the above example, your time is leveraged. For every hour of work you do personally, there are three, or five, or even twenty hours of work being done for your client. Your projects are no longer limited by your available time, and your business is free to earn a much greater amount of money. To truly get the most out of freelancing, you need to hire and work with other people.

Applying Leverage to Your Business

How you use the concept of leveraging and other people in your own business will depend on two factors: what type of business you have and what goals you have for your business.

Almost every freelance business can benefit from a hired team, but how you implement that team is going to be different from one company to the next.

If your business relies heavily on specialized knowledge, for example, you will want to create a team that allows you to focus 100% of your time applying your knowledge. You should outsource or hire other people to handle all of the non-specialized tasks.

If your business is made up of more standardized work, such as a design business, it's possible to build a team that handles almost every aspect of the business. Which projects you keep for yourself will depend on what you like to do best.

How big you want to grow your business will also dictate how you should approach building a team. The larger you eventually want to grow, the more aggressively you will need to hire out. The more you leverage your time, the faster and bigger you'll be able to grow.

On the other hand, if your goal is to create a small freelance business, then you can outsource fewer tasks and use your team to augment your own abilities, not replace them.

The Distributed Team Concept

Unlike larger companies, we freelancers have no need to hire employees in-house or full-time. In fact, most freelancers couldn't do that anyway.

That's where the concept of a distributed team comes into play. Imagine a team made up of outsourced help, virtual assistants, and other freelancers – distributed around the globe. With the right combination of these groups, you can create a team that works completely on-demand, costs nothing when you aren't using it, and is scalable to accept as much or as little work as you need. There is almost no barrier to entry and an enormous amount of flexibility.

As freelancers, we are uniquely positioned to benefit from this. We have the talent, skill, and independence to run and grow a thriving business, but it is incredibly difficult to make the jump from a one-person company to a small business with an office and employees. Creating a distributed freelance team eliminates this problem and allows any freelancer to grow fluidly from a small company to a much larger one.

The Parts of Your Team

Creating a freelance team requires taking a number of different people with a variety of skills and organizing them into a group that can easily handle your projects and help your business grow.

The first part of creating that group is to examine the different building blocks you have available, and see which you want to use in your team.

There are three types of relationships that we recommend and discuss in this book: outsourcing, cross-sourcing, and partnerships. Within each of these different groups, there are many different types of people with a large variety of costs and skills. Let's take a closer look at those different groups, and the type of people that you can hire in each.

Outsourcing

Outsourcing is a term generally applied to inexpensive, generalized workers that you can use to perform many of the easier and more time-consuming aspects of your business. Most of these outsourced workers are a part of a firm specifically dedicated to outsourcing. Some of the most common types of outsourcing include:

- Call Centers
- Budget Virtual Assistants
- Technical Support
- Data Entry Specialists
- Computer Programmers

It's important to consider that you will find both high and low quality service through outsourcing, and you shouldn't expect a $10/hr programmer to compete with someone charging $50/hr.

Cross-Sourcing

Cross-sourcing is similar to outsourcing, and many would even call them the same thing, but we'd like to make an important distinction: outsourcing is hiring someone with a different and often less expensive skill, whereas cross-sourcing is hiring someone with a similar or equivalent skill. Outsourcing is typically done through a firm or larger company, whereas cross-sourcing is frequently done with other freelancers.

Some cross-sourcing examples include:

- Web Designers or Developers
- Premium Virtual Assistants
- Copywriters
- Graphic Designers
- Marketers

Partnerships

Partnering is a very different type of arrangement from outsourcing or cross-sourcing. In a partnership, both members are on equal footing and work is done on a percentage or ownership basis rather than a fixed or hourly price. Sometimes there is no cost involved at all and, instead, the partnership involves exchanging tasks or favors.

There are many different types of partnerships, a few of the most common include:

- Venture Partnership
- Referral Partnership
- White-label or Resale Partnership
- Single Project Partnership

It's best to get a full understanding of these types before deciding how to organize and use them in your business. The following chapters will discuss the three types in more detail, but before we get into that, let's look at some more reasons to work with other people.

Five Reasons to Work with Others

1. **Successful people have support teams.**
   Few successful people become that way on their own, and even those who start out alone eventually have to get support from other people in order to remain successful.

   Behind every great person and every brilliant mind, you'll find a full network helping to support that greatness and allow the individual to do even greater things.

2. **It's easy to get started.**
   These strategies don't require you to spend a huge amount of money or hire someone full-time. The barrier to entry is very low, and you can get started in as little as a few hours.

3. **You can help others as well as yourself.**
   One of the best parts about working with other people is that you will benefit them, too, by creating a mutually beneficial situation where everyone works together to reach goals. When you're alone and doing it all on your own, you work a lot harder than you need to.

4. **Your team will be incredibly scalable.**
   One month, you may only require one virtual assistant for a few hours; but the next month, you need a couple programmers for a full week. By creating connections with different types of people, it's possible for you to scale your endeavors to incredible heights.

5. **Benefit the freelancing industry.**
   By hiring and working with other freelancers, you will increase the prominence and prosperity of the entire industry. Freelancers joining together are a powerful force.

Tapping into the power of people is a smart way to grow your business. People can help you by taking over the work that you don't have the skills for or the tasks that you don't enjoy doing. Let's use an example. Let's say that you decide to create an informational product so that you can sell it and enjoy some passive income. How will you reach that goal?

A solo freelancer with no relationships with others will have to conceive the idea, outline the plan, write the content, put it into proper format, figure out how to sell it, market the product, stir up a buzz, deliver it to buyers, collect money, and track payments.

That's a lot of work for one person to handle, especially when that person still needs to work on client projects to keep the business going. Often, expanding your team/network may be the only way to grow.

Who Do You Want to Work With?

When creating your team you'll need to decide what type of professionals you'd like to work with, and who would provide the most benefits to you and your business.

Would you like to collaborate with:

- **Someone who offers identical services?** You could increase production of what you already sell. For example, a website designer could collaborate with another designer.

- **Someone who offers related services?**
  You could add new services to the ones that you offer. For example, a sales copywriter might work with a press release writer.

- **Someone with services in a related industry?**
  You could create a one-stop shop for clients. For example, a content writer or a coder might be likely professionals to work within your graphic design business.

- **Someone who can handle various small tasks?**
  You could reduce your administration workload. For example, a virtual assistant can work in any industry to help increase efficiency and your free time.

- **Someone who can improve your business?**
  You could work with people who can provide you with what you need now so that you can get ahead faster in business.

You need to know what you need and in which direction you want to go before you begin the process of finding team members. You have to be aware of the personal goals you'd like to reach, the achievements you'd like to make, and the priorities that really matter in your life. Only then can you find exactly who you need to work with to get what you want.

Ideas for Using Your Team

Working with other people is a smart way of getting work done faster, whether you hire them on a per project basis or collaborate together to achieve results.

You can outsource some of your administrative tasks to gain free time or you can cross-source part of a big client project. You could even partner with another company to take on a project that is gigantic.

How can you use other people in your business? Here are some quick ideas to start you in the right direction:

Overhaul or Upgrade Your Site

You can easily outsource a site overhaul to a good specialist, even if creating websites is your specialty. The cost is a one-time expense, and the rewards are worthwhile. You'll save time and also increase your business potential to attract new customers, which means the site overhaul pays for itself.

Update Your Marketing Materials

This is another great item to hire out and one that can boost your business potential quickly. You could even hire an entire marketing business that can take care of all your needs without having to manage different people.

Create Stuff You Can Sell

Hire people who can create revenue-generating products that you can sell on your site. It's a good way to get some passive income while you're busy focusing on other areas of your business.

Add Talent to a Project

When you aren't sure of what you're doing, don't have the proper skills, or can only do an amateur job at best, definitely consider cross-sourcing to another freelancer who has those talents. Trying to do the work yourself may end up causing a lot of headaches due to a mistake or an oversight.

Outsource Routine Tasks

A task that continually crops up in your business and that never really changes is a task that should be outsourced. Data-entry, for example, can become very rote and boring. Write down the instructions and get someone to do the work for you.

You can look for outsourcing opportunities in your accounting, administration, and project setup. Outsource the more basic tasks that are the same for each project and take over when the foundation is ready for you to do your magic.

The best tasks to outsource are ones that really don't require your supervision. If you just want a task completed, and you don't particularly care how it gets done, outsource it. Your supervision over the process won't be required, and that's perfect when results are all you want to see.

Streamline Your Projects

If you can outsource or hire another freelancer to do parts of a client project that you don't want to do, then you should. It will increase your output substantially and allow you to take on more projects. For example, if the websites you design could be produced more rapidly by outsourcing the basic layout creation, it might be worthwhile in order to increase the overall capacity of your business.

Take-away Message:

The best places to hire other people are the tasks that are either basic, repetitive, or will directly help your business grow. Choosing the type of hiring relationship or partnership will depend on the complexity and difficulty of the task and on your goals for the relationship.

Outsourcing

There are many types of outsourcing, some of which will prove extremely useful to your business. Outsourcing is a very cost-effective way to handle some of the easier and more routine tasks of a freelance business.

Outsourced virtual assistants can perform tasks such as online research, scheduling appointments, or data entry. Some of the more expensive virtual assistants can handle a multitude of tasks and systems, including managing an entire project and its required vendors.

Overall, outsourcing is a great way to free up your own time for the more complex or detailed work involved in your business. You can also delegate any of the tasks that you just don't like to do.

Before we get into the details of which areas of your team are best suited to outsourcing, let's take a minute to clear up some of the many outsourcing myths.

Seven Myths About Outsourcing

Tim Ferris launched outsourcing into the spotlight with his bestseller book, *The Four Hour Workweek*. He demonstrated how easy it is to outsource almost anything and live a life of complete freedom.

Outsourcing isn't new, though. For centuries, people have been hiring others to do the jobs they can't or don't want to do. Kings commissioned army generals, minstrels, and cooks. International businesses outsource to design studios, consultants and engineers. General contractors outsource to plumbers, carpenters and architects.

No, outsourcing isn't new. But what is new is that outsourcing is gaining a bad reputation, and in many cases that bad reputation is based on false information.

We're going to shatter seven myths surrounding outsourcing, because we feel that too many people are cheating themselves out of a better life by shunning this opportunity to work less and make more money.

1. **Myth: Outsourcing Means Hiring Cheap Labor**
   Some people associate outsourcing with cheap labor. The truth is that outsourcing simply means having a service or function completed by someone outside your business. You transfer the responsibility of getting the job done to someone else.

   The cost related to contracting someone else to complete that function or service is irrelevant. You don't have to hire sweatshop laborers if you don't want to.

2. **Myth: Outsourcing Causes People to Lose Jobs**
   Many people have lost their jobs to outsourcing. Companies trying to cut costs have shut down departments and contracted independent businesses to perform company functions. That certainly does tend to create hard feelings and we sympathize with those who lost their jobs.

   Outsourcing, however, does not create job loss; it creates a cash-flow shift (or job shift).

   For a more concrete definition for outsourcing, the Heritage Foundation puts it best:

   > *Outsourcing is a means of getting more final output with lower cost inputs, which leads to lower prices for all U.S. firms and families. Lower prices lead directly to higher standards of living and more jobs in a growing economy.*

   A lower cost of goods means more money in people's pockets. More money in people's pockets means increased spending. The more we spend, the more providers need to fill demand. The higher the demand, the more jobs are created to meet those needs.

3. **Myth: Outsourcing Equals Cheap Quality**
   Some people believe that the minute you outsource, you're getting sub-standard quality in return. The truth is that outsourcing *can* result in cheap quality,

but just as often, it results in very high quality services.

This myth came into being because people frequently don't research the skill level of the providers they hire. They aren't satisfied with the results, and they make sweeping generalizations about outsourcing at large.

Any time that you contract with someone to complete a service or create a product, you should always invest some time into checking references, examining portfolios for quality, and asking about skill levels. Good providers have a clear record of accomplishment and strong references.

4. **Myth: Outsourcing Means Hiring Overseas**
   Some people prefer to support local economies and businesses, and they frequently associate outsourcing with overseas providers. While there are many outsourcing firms located all around the world, there are also many local outsourcing providers as well.

   If you prefer to outsource locally, finding a good provider for your needs is as easy as finding a business located in your area, region, or country that offers the services you require. You don't have to hire overseas providers if you don't want to.

5. **Myth: Outsourcing Lowers Market Values**
   Some people feel that outsourcing drives down the market value of the service they offer or the product they sell. They see that many outsourcing firms have cheaper rates, and they feel that these low rates affect their potential to charge more. In short, they're afraid outsourcing causes price wars and rate competition.

   Anyone who offers the same service or product as you do is your competition, whether they are considered outsourcers or not. In fact, *you* may be considered *their* competition, because clients outsource projects to you, don't they?

   Price tags have very little to do with outsourcing, though. So many factors influence rates, market value, and pricing, including (and certainly not limited to) quality, scarcity, demand, expertise, skills, production methods... the list goes on and on. The act of outsourcing affects pricing very little, if at all.

6. **Myth: Outsourcing Means Loss of Control**
   Some people prefer not to outsource because they're afraid they'll lose control. The job won't be done as they would do it. Many freelancers feel that only they can do their job, and no one else could possibly do the same.

   Keep this in mind: if you can't be replaced, than you can never be promoted. Think of Donald Trump, the multimillionaire. Does he perform every task in each of his businesses?

The truth is that many of the tasks you do can be done by someone else, if you've established and documented a clear system and process that tells them exactly how to do it and the results you seek.

Outsourcing doesn't mean someone else has control of your business, it means that you delegate *completion* of the task. In short, if you need the task done, *how* it gets done should be irrelevant.

7. **Myth: Outsourcing is Hard to Set Up**
   Outsourcing firms are very skilled at gathering the information they need to get started quickly. After all, their job is to help you. Outsourced providers can take the simplest, "I need help but don't know where to start," and turn that into suggestions, improvements, and solutions.

   Remember that outsourced help is made up of people whose service is to serve you, no matter what your needs. Designers can help you create the right look, marketers can help you gain new clients, writers can help you convey the perfect message... whatever you need, they're there to help.

8. **Bonus Myth: Outsourcing is Expensive**
   Some people need – very much so – to keep costs and expenses as low as possible. They feel that they can't afford to hire someone else to take over a task, so they do the work themselves. As the saying goes, time is money. Why waste time when you can use it to earn more money?

   The problem is that many freelancers make the common mistake of focusing on the loss of profits and the cost of outsourcing without considering the bigger picture: the value of your personal time is much higher than the cost of outsourcing.

   For example, a website designer may earn $1,000 per design. Let's say that outsourcing to another designer for the same results would cost $500. That's a loss of $500 on profits, right?

   Not exactly. If it takes the designer 10 hours to produce one design, and someone else works those 10 hours, then the designer could take on a second, third, and fourth design project instead of just the one.

   That means the designer ends up creating revenues of $2000 by outsourcing instead of the $1,000 he'd receive if he'd done the work himself. He didn't lose money. In fact, he increased his profits by 100%, or $1000.

> "If you want to work smarter instead of harder it makes sense to hire help. With a virtual assistant you need never worry about long-term contracts, renting an office, or struggling with the dismal idea of paying a fortune…"
>
> *Nick Cernis, PutThingsOff and Wordprezzie.com*

Consider what you could do if you outsourced 10 hours of work:

- You could market your business and gain new clients who will become loyal, long-term customers.

- You could focus on creating a passive income source that earns you money independently after you release it to the market.

- You could work for your existing clients and earn revenue at a higher rate than the cost of the outsourcing.

These are just suggestions, but the point is clear: outsourcing lowers costs, saves time, increases revenues, gets work done faster, increases your client base, and makes you more money.

Fitting Outsourcing into Your Team

Outsourcing provides an excellent means to handle smaller, repetitive, and routine tasks. Any task that you can create a detailed outline of how to do, you can outsource.

Remember that using inexpensive providers can produce inexpensive results, so take that into account when looking for an outsourcing firm to use. The amount of high-level judgment and creative thinking your tasks require will dictate how much you should be spending on your provider.

We recommend outsourcing tasks that have a very definitive final result. That way you can outsource with the confidence of knowing that when the task is done, it will be done properly. More creative or difficult tasks that have a subjective result are going to be better handled through cross-sourcing or more expensive providers.

Take-away Message:

There are lots of different options to consider when choosing how to outsource certain tasks or projects. Some methods may seem less cost effective at first, but will turn out to be a great way to leverage your free time.

Always keep the bigger picture in mind. Know the costs of outsourcing, but also know what you gain through outsourcing, such as potential growth and more free time.

Cross-Sourcing and Hiring Freelancers

Cross-sourcing is when you hire an otherwise equal freelancer to complete a task for your business. It's not the same as partnering, because you will actually be paying this person, and they become a part of your team. It differs from outsourcing in that these team members will be able to handle more difficult tasks, frequently even things you yourself could not do yourself.

There are many reasons you should consider doing this. Perhaps you've had a larger-than-usual number of clients this month, and you didn't want to turn anyone away. With cross-sourcing, you could delegate these projects to another freelancer, one you trust to do a good job, and you'll still maintain your client relationship and some of the income – even though you're not completing the project yourself.

To take this a step further, cross-sourcing can help smooth the highs and lows of freelancing, and ultimately help you build a business that can handle hundreds of projects at once. If you work with a few different people, you can minimize the dry spouts and capitalize on the floods. When you've completely set up your team, and have several providers to work with, you'll be able to take on as much work as you can manage.

In a cross-sourcing relationship you keep all of your client contacts and will probably handle all communications with the client. The client doesn't need to know that you're sending his/her work to another business.

Cross-sourcing is also an excellent boost to the freelancing community. By hiring other freelancers, you benefit everyone in the process and give others more work to do. You can also take on more work yourself, which raises the overall profile of the freelance community.

Here are some things you can do with cross-sourcing:

- Skilled graphic design
- Basic or advanced programming
- Copywriting, ebook authoring, and blogging
- Web design and development
- Project management and oversight
- Many more...

The limits of what you can do by combining the talents of other freelancers are nearly nonexistent. With the right combination, you will have a very powerful team that's capable of handling anything. You and your business can enter new fields, take on more work, and add to the selection of services you provide to your clients.

When to Use Cross-Sourcing

While there aren't any major drawbacks to cross-sourcing, there are a few things you should be aware of before hiring other freelancers.

Cross-sourcing tends to be more expensive than outsourcing, because the workers are more skilled. This doesn't mean that the overall cost of a project will increase if you hire another freelancer. Often times a more skilled worker can complete a task in less time.

It does mean that you should consider which tasks you hire other freelancers for and which you send to an outsourcing firm. Tasks that require little skill or creative thought should be outsourced to a company that can complete them very inexpensively. Tasks that require a lot of creativity, independence, and skill should be sent to a freelancer who can handle the job effectively.

Take data entry, for example. Something as repetitive and easy to do as data entry should be outsourced as opposed to cross-sourced. It's a somewhat monotonous and long job and would be very expensive if you hired a skilled worker to do it.

Looking at the other side of this, a cross-sourced freelancer can handle jobs that are much more complicated and advanced than an outsourced provider, and they can do so with the highest quality and creativity standards. You can safely send just about any job to the right cross-sourced freelancer.

In an ideal situation, you could hire an outsourcing firm to handle the basic and repetitive tasks, and you can use your more advanced freelancers to handle the creative or difficult work that needs a much higher quality standard. This way you get the best of both worlds.

You could even have your advanced team members manage your outsourced providers, and the whole project could take place with little need of you or your time. You could go on vacation, and your client projects would progress meaningfully onward without your presence.

> ***Take-away Message:***
>
> ***Cross-sourcing and referral partnerships are a great way for like-minded freelancers to leverage each other's abilities. You can choose the formality of the relationship and change it as the needs of your businesses expand.***
>
> ***Your clients benefit from these relationships as well, because they do not need to find a new vendor for their project. Instead, they can rely on your judgment on how to get the job done and continue to come to you for their future needs.***

Partnering

In a partnership, the goal is not to hire someone to complete an existing project but to work together with another freelancer or business on a new venture where both of you benefit. You can partner with people for a very wide range of activities, everything from a simple agreement to share a resource all the way to a partnership on an entirely new business.

Partnering takes advantage of the strengths and resources of each participant and combines them in a way that benefits the whole. The workload and benefits are distributed to everyone involved in the partnership.

Growth Partnerships

Let's take a look at a specific example. Imagine a freelancer who wants to develop a new asset – let's say an eBook. That person, and others, could easily benefit from a growth partnership. A writer, a graphic designer, and a marketing consultant can collaborate to create the final product. One person writes. The other adds graphics. A third sets up the sales page. Together, they market and split the profits three ways.

Each person has a task to do, no one becomes overwhelmed, and the product hits the market faster. It's well made, well marketed, and everyone benefits from the sales. This is an example of a growth partnership.

There are several advantages to growth partnerships:

- The workload for each partner is manageable
- Specific skills and talents are applied where needed
- A wider pool of expertise goes into the venture
- More people are available to help sell the product
- You could complete a product or start a business that you might not be able to alone

A growth partnership can help you build an additional income stream while you work on client projects, an entirely new business in your spare time, or a non-profit initiative that you can't afford to do on your own. It's the perfect answer to the problem of *wanting* to do something but not having the time or resources available to do so.

Marketing Partnerships

Marketing partnerships are similar to growth partnerships in the fact that you're dealing with another freelancer, but instead of collaborating on a new project, you are working to increase the sales of your separate, existing companies. In this type of partnership, you might be referring clients, promoting each other's products, or sharing the cost of expensive advertising.

While it may seem silly to share your marketing efforts with another business, potentially even one that you compete with, marketing partnerships are actually a very smart strategy. Together, your respective companies can to increase their reach and prominence to a degree that neither of you would have been able to do individually.

The result is that both of your businesses will get more clients and be more successful.

The advantages of a marketing partnership are:

- It can start as a casual relationship and become more formal later on

- Each partner uses his or her available resources, and together they work for the good of both companies

- Each partner can share clients with the other, and both companies will get more work than otherwise

- The partnership can afford advertising and opportunities that the individual companies could not

In short, everyone lends their skills and resources for the mutual benefit of both companies. Partners can refer clients back and forth, market each other's services, and simultaneously grow both businesses. It is a winning situation for all.

Single-Project Partnerships

A single project partnership is the same as the other types of partnerships except for a different timeframe and purpose. The goal of a single-project partnership is to combine the skills of both or all of the parties involved to take on a specific project they would otherwise have not been able to do.

These projects are generally larger client projects that involve work in many different areas. A single freelancer or business may not have the capability to complete the project and would have to turn it down if it weren't for the other partners. Because of the partnership, everyone benefits from the shared resources of the individuals.

The advantage of a single-project partnership is that, by collaborating, the group can take on new and larger work and thus make each of the individual companies more profitable.

Take-away Message:

Solo freelancers often don't have the ability to accomplish everything they'd like to do by themselves. There just isn't enough time, resources, or energy available.

Partnering with other people can help you attain your goals faster, take on new projects that you don't have time for on your own, and even reach for opportunities that would otherwise be unavailable to you. Everyone involved in a partnership will benefit from the combined strength of the individuals for their future needs.

Hiring, Firing, and Management

Finding people to work with you, and for you, is relatively easy thanks to the internet and the wealth of skilled professionals available on the web.

You can outsource, you can find a partner, you can hire a team, or you can create joint ventures. You can buy white-label products from a provider or you can use marketing partnerships to get more clients.

There are all sorts of ways to work with others, and there are all sorts of people available to work with – how you go about doing that is the question. Which person is the right person? How do you find good people to help your business? How do you choose where each person belongs?

Finding Good People

No matter what business you are in, you should ideally work with people who are:

- Reliable
- Dependable
- Cost-effective
- Skilled
- Open-minded

- Fast
- Friendly
- Organized
- Trustworthy

Other qualities are admirable or might fit well with your needs, but these basic qualities are must-have requirements for anyone you want on your team. The person who has these qualities would be a definite asset to your business.

The Meet and Greet

You know who you need to work with and the qualities they should have – now you need to find them. Where are these dedicated, reliable workers?

Here are a few ways to scout them out:

- Advertise – post a want ad on your site or on freelance job boards

- Network – ask people if they know of anyone who might be interested

- Headhunt – find people whose work you like and ask if they're interested in working with you

Keep your eyes open, ask around, and let people know you're looking for someone to collaborate with.

"Skills are overrated. Perfect products delivered past deadline kill companies faster than decent products delivered on-time. Test someone's ability to deliver on a specific and tight deadline before hiring them based on a dazzling portfolio."

Time Ferris, Author of 4-Hour Work Week

No matter how you find candidates for collaboration, you need to spend time discussing, communicating, and getting a good idea of what you can expect from each person.

And when we say spend time, we mean more than a few emails or a phone call. Get a feel for the type of person you are dealing with. Try to learn more about his or her business values and ethics, the response time you might expect from them, and the level of professionalism that the person upholds.

You need to be comfortable with this person before you start to work together. Taking time to get to know each other will give both of you a good idea of the relationship you might have in business.

A warning:
Desperate people do make for instant help. They also often make the worst workers. If they aren't working now, there may be good reason. Be cautious.

Another warning:
It's nice to give people a break or a chance, and it's good to be kind and helpful. Keep in mind that you have a business to run and customers to satisfy. If you're thinking of working with someone inexperienced with the intention of mentoring or training the individual, then be ready to step in and take over when needed.

Other Hiring Factors

There are a lot of really nice people out there who you might love to add to your team – but that isn't always the best idea. There are several other considerations to factor into your selection of whom to collaborate with, including:

- Cost
- Communication
- Cultural differences
- Time zone

Let's look at each factor a little closer.

Cost

Cost is probably one of the most important factors in choosing a person to hire. Finding people who can help you earn profits and create a better business is key.

International business has some specific economical advantages, because people often charge rates that fit the market value of their local economy. This creates the potential for some substantial savings if you are interested in hiring overseas.

On the other hand, cost often (but not always) indicates the quality of the work you will receive. Sometimes hiring an expert will seem to cost more but will actually be a substantially better choice for your overall goals.

Communication

Another important factor in selecting people to work with involves how well those individuals communicate – and by how well they communicate, we mean not only verbally or in writing, but also in their ability to grasp and convey concepts, manners, and professionalism.

These communication problems can happen to anyone, so be careful of prejudices. Many people mistakenly believe that those with English as a second language aren't proficient in communication and can't be understood.

We've met people in many countries who write, speak, and communicate better than our neighbors do. Country of origin does not determine ability to communicate.

Cultural Differences

Cultural differences can cause problems in relationships – and more easily than you'd think.

What's perfectly fine to one person might be offensive to someone living in another country. Jokes can become insults, tone of voice can become offensive, and a style of writing can cause upset. Of course, there are also big faux pas, like discussing religion, politics, or sensitive moral issues.

In business, the best rule of thumb is to avoid sensitive subjects and be aware that cultural differences can create issues. The best way to handle them when they do arise is to have an open mind and understand that other people were not raised in the same manner that you were.

Time Zones

A last factor in your decision on who to work with involves time zones. It's easy to collaborate thanks to the internet, but how will time zones affect your business?

What do you do when it's noon in your location but midnight where the other person lives? How will you handle operations when your marketer is having breakfast, you're enjoying an afternoon break, and your web designer is just getting ready for bed? Where do you all meet up?

Different time zones aren't deal-breakers, and there are actually ways to make time zone differences work in your favor.

For example, one of the advantages of working with someone in a different time zone is that they work while you sleep, presenting you with results in the morning so that you can make good progress with your day. Throughout the day, you can build up a list of tasks and to-dos, send them off, and enjoy your evening knowing the work is all being taken care of.

One of the disadvantages of working from different time zones is that you may not be able to communicate directly with these people at certain moments in the day. This means you may have to wait for answers, which could slow down your business or require changes to how you work for smoother operation.

In all cases, good planning, proper time management, effective use of communication, and foresight are key.

And when you have good systems, smart processes, and turnaround times for clients that take time zone differences into consideration (with a little extra time padding in case of emergencies), you can work with anyone easily and effectively with the least amount of stress.

Take-away Message:

When choosing people for your team, get to know their personality, work ethics, and strengths. Until you've acquainted yourself with them, you cannot be sure whether or not he/she is a good fit for your business.

10 Ways to Build Relationships

Working with other people is a great deal of fun. Teamwork can be productive, fulfilling, and enjoyable.

There are still going to be some off days, though. You may sometimes feel that you just can't convey your thoughts well. You might have days when no one seems to understand each other. You'll certainly have days when you feel tired and cranky.

Working with other people isn't always easy, so here are some ways to help create great relationships:

Reward people

Tell people when they have done a good job or when you're pleased with a particular element of the project.

Reward people more

Sometimes, a little bonus can be just the thing to show appreciation. You can give people a monetary bonus from time to time, or send a gift certificate to say thanks.

Relax

Develop a good, friendly relationship with providers and collaborators. Joke a little, lighten up and talk about fun stuff from time to time.

Be prompt

Always take care of the people who work with you. Answer their requests or questions quickly so that they can continue progressing at a good pace.

Be a team player

It's important that the people you choose to work with know that you're on their side. Be ready to stand up for people you work with and stick by them. Respect their opinions and accept when they need you to take a stand on their behalf.

Accept feedback

Some of the best ideas, suggestions, and feedback come from people who know about your business. Ask for feedback and welcome suggestions when they present themselves.

Offer feedback

If you spot an improvement that could help someone else's business or ways of working, share it.

Give testimonials

A nice surprise for the people who work with you is a testimonial about their products or services. A testimonial helps support other businesses that may be able to give back to you. By vouching and recommending others, you also encourage them to do the same for you.

Be sympathetic

Life isn't always roses and sunshine. When you work with others, you'll sometimes learn that they're going through a rough patch or a temporary hard time. Show sympathy and understanding.

> "Dealing with people is probably the biggest problem you face, especially if you are in business. Yes, and that is also true if you are a housewife, architect or engineer."
>
> *Dale Carnegie, Author of How to Win Friends and Influence People*

Take a day off

Don't overlook the value of free time for play. If the people you work with are local, head out with them for a day at the go-kart tracks or visit a theme park together.

There are plenty of ways to bolster positive relationships and create a good working environment with the people on your team. Think of others as much as you do yourself, be ready to be helpful and kind, and give first without expecting anything back.

How to Give Good Feedback

Giving feedback to collaborators, providers, and team members may be a new situation for you. Freelancers commonly receive feedback from clients and understand its value to a good job – but you may not have been in the position of having to give feedback to others.

It can be difficult to know how to give good feedback to people you work with. Should you praise constantly? Should you only praise the remarkable? And what about when you have to say you don't like something? It's tough to know what to say, and many people avoid saying anything at all.

It's okay to give feedback. You're not judging a person's worth or ability – you're simply telling them your preferences, guiding them to get the results you need, and offering suggestions for improvements.

Here are some tips on how to give feedback in a positive way, even when the feedback is negative:

- When something needs to be said, say it. Add a disclaimer if that helps. "Jack, we're pretty good friends, but I need to talk to you about business for a minute." This helps the person make the distinction between friendship and business, and show that you're separating the two relationships.

- Avoid all "you" phrases, especially when asking the person to revise his or her work. "You" comes off as a personal attack and puts people on the defensive. For example, stay away from sentences like, "You should use more adjectives and color in your writing," or "You have to stop using so much blue in designs."

- How to you avoid "you"? Remove the focus from the person and put it on the service or product. "The writing could use more adjectives and color," for example, or, "It'd be great to see some more red in designs." That conveys suggestions for improvement and your preferences, and the person doesn't feel attacked.

- Sandwich negative feedback between two positive comments. The positive introductory comment puts the person in a more receptive frame of mind, and they'll be more likely to be open to the negative feedback.

- Another trick is to finish off discussions with, "What do you think?" This gives the other person the opportunity to agree or disagree with your comments, while leaving room for the individual to add his or her own thoughts. People like being asked for their opinion, and it makes them feel valuable to know that you want to hear those thoughts.

- Show that you make mistakes too. "I wanted to point something out to you, because I used to do this in the past and discovered that there's a better way." This conveys that you are an equal and no better than the other person. It makes them feel more comfortable to know that they're not the only one who makes mistakes.

- Leave the door open. "If you want to talk about this some more or share your thoughts, just let me know. I appreciate any ideas that will make this project rock." Letting people know that you're open to their thoughts conveys that you're willing to listen to what they have to say – and everyone likes to be heard.

Learning how to give good feedback is a bit of an art. Some people are more receptive to certain methods than others. Some like heavy feedback and really being picked apart; most enjoy gentle feedback and compassion.

Everyone enjoys knowing that they're valuable. Feedback tells them how they can be even better, both for themselves and for your projects.

Communicating With Your Team

Communicating with your team is something you'll need to spend time learning how to do best. Some team members will work differently than others, and you will need to learn about each and adapt your style.

Over-Communication

When you first start collaborating with others, you may want to make sure that you share as much information as possible with the other person (or people). However, this can easily lead to giving too much information.

Over-communication is a problem when giving instructions. Too much information forces people to sift through fluff, unimportant data, and irrelevant details to sort out the relevant, pertinent information they need.

That wastes time, and it can lead to a mess of issues:

- People become overwhelmed when faced with too much information

- Skimming and scanning long text means crucial details might be overlooked or skipped

- Task prioritization may not be appropriate due to the recipient's inaccurate perception of importance

- Misunderstandings or miscommunications need to be corrected, wasting time, lowering profits, and costing money

Here are some tips to help prevent over-communication and give people the information they need so that projects are smooth and simple:

- Keep instructions concise and clear
- Break down information into manageable chunks
- Use bullet points and short sentences
- Make sure to list project requirements
- Avoid including details that aren't relevant
- Create a checklist of tasks or action items
- List project priorities in order of importance
- Clearly indicate any deadlines or dates

Lastly, make sure that the people working with you know they can (and should) ask questions, get clarification, and confirm details. Two-way communication is vital to getting the best results.

Under-Communication

Many people have the opposite problem of over-communicators: some people don't share enough key information. A lack of information can derail a project and cause some serious breakdowns, both of which cost your business time and money, not to mention clients.

People who don't have enough information may be unsure of requirements or needs. They might have to guess at what they should do. They lack details and can't complete the task to high standards, or they miss crucial data to do a good job.

Under-communication wastes time, energy and money. Basically, people who don't have enough information and the right information can't do a good job.

People under-communicate for many reasons:

- Attempting to avoid over-communication
- A fear of losing a client to another provider
- A lack of knowledge about the information necessary to do a good job
- A heavy hand in cutting out irrelevant information
- Being rushed to get an e-mail or phone call completed

Provide workers with key details, especially all those that influence the results or delivery of the project. Give people the resources, information, and tools they need to do their job well – because the better they do, the more success you'll achieve.

Tips for Working with Others

Collaboration lets you leverage available resources to get more done in less time, and it allows you to shift away from the work you don't want to do so that you can concentrate on what you want – and need – to do.

Communicating effectively with the people you collaborate helps reduce problems that might arise. Good systems and clear processes increase the chance of smooth progress. Applications that assist collaboration and communication are fantastic, too.

Collaborating with others isn't always easy, though. There will be hiccups and bumps along the way, especially when you first start collaborating. Mistakes might happen, misunderstandings might occur, and that's to be expected. Everyone's human, after all.

Problems don't have to happen frequently, though, and there are ways that you can reduce the likelihood of them happening at all. Good business practices can make the experience of collaboration a great one.

Here are some tips on how to avoid problems when collaborating, and some ways make sure the teamwork experience is positive for all involved.

1. Give Frequent Feedback

Too many people have a fear of giving feedback. They say nothing, building up complaints, and then shock the person by revealing a long list of dissatisfactions.

This is a huge mistake – continual feedback, both positive and negative, is integral to improved results, a good working environment, and a pleasant relationship. Remember, no one reads minds, so be clear and forthcoming with feedback.

Of course, when giving negative feedback, do so politely and with diplomacy. Give workers the tools to correct the situation, too. Offer specific thoughts and concrete points about what you'd like changed. Provide ideas and suggestions for improvement.

2. Look To Yourself First

When there is a problem, always look to yourself first. People interpret information differently, so possibly what you believed to be clear and understood was misinterpreted or perceived differently than you intended.

In fact, much of our communication involves subjective perception. We all have different views, understandings, and interpretations.

So ask yourself: Did you communicate clearly? Was the miscommunication because of subjective perception? Did you over- or under-communicate or were your instructions open to personal interpretation? What could you have communicated differently that would have been better?

3. Focus on Solutions

When a problem arises, all that matters is resolving it quickly and efficiently. Focus on correcting the situation and finding a solution instead of concentrating on the cause of problem or laying blame.

Write options for solutions down and share them with others. Ask if they see other solutions that might be better. Teamwork means being able to work together when something goes wrong just as much as it means being able to work together when everything is right.

Also, examine your systems and business processes to see if the problem occurred because of a fault the system. Would using a different method of working be better for the future? Is there another way of collaborating or sharing information that would have prevented the issue from occurring? Are there improvements that could be made to your business?

4. Everyone Gets a Second Chance

We're all human, and everyone screws up now and again. That's important to acknowledge and accept. Because we're only human and make mistakes, we also deserve a chance to remedy the situation and get a second shot at the task or project.

In many cases, presenting a situation summary and a checklist of action items to the people involved has good results. Telling someone, "Here's where we are; here's what we need to do," is often all it takes for the person to say, "Ahhh, I see now!"

There will be bumps in the road with any project, no matter who is involved. Mistakes and miscommunications aren't limited to rookies or beginners, and even the experts trip up sometimes. The best thing you can do is to keep learning and approach collaboration with an open mind.

Take Away Message:

Working with a variety of people can be difficult, and everyone has their own strengths and weaknesses, but there are ways you can communicate effectively. Be open to other people's points of view, and focus on learning to become a better manager. Over time, you will learn what it takes to communicate effectively and manage a fantastic team.

How to Terminate a Relationship

We've covered some ways to communicate well with the people you work with. We've also covered tips on how to improve the working relationship. Sometimes, though, things just don't work out.

Ending a business relationship with someone you've been working with can be very difficult. It's sometimes a necessary action because your business needs this to happen, but it is always an emotional situation that can be very uncomfortable.

As a freelancer, however, you are most likely not the person's direct employer, which is beneficial for both of you. He/she most likely has other clients or partners that provide income, so you're not destroying his/her livelihood. Terminating your relationship with someone is therefore much less difficult than if they were your employee.

Before you decide that you're not going to use a person's services or products anymore, get in touch with them to discuss the situation. In many cases, a simple miscommunication is the cause.

Be sure that you've been clear, and that there was no room for personal interpretation of your requirements, too. Look over past communications, your requests, the tone you used, and determine if you were clear.

Did you share all the information the person needed to do a good job? Was there anything you left out or forgot to mention? Have you provided fair warning to the person? Terminations that come as a surprise or as sudden arbitrary decisions can put your business at risk.

If you've thought it over and you still want to terminate the relationship, you need to move towards protecting yourself and your business.

Put it in writing

Draft what you want to say before you speak or write to the other person. Use non-confrontational and neutral language.

It's usually better to write the person a letter or email than to speak on the telephone. A paper trail (even virtual email paper) removes potential misunderstanding and confusion. Letters give people something to refer back to and show that you've done what you needed to do.

Get Acknowledgement of feedback

Ask the person to respond and confirm your letter by a certain day. Of course, give the individual the time he or she needs to think over your comments and a chance to respond.

Be exceedingly fair

Don't hold back on unpaid wages, don't try to punish someone, and do fulfill your end of the agreement up to the point of termination. Forcing a person to compensate you for any losses isn't a good course of action.

Be clear about your reasons

Don't rehash the past, but do provide bullet points to make sure there isn't any confusion. Tell people the truth and don't leave them guessing.

Allow them a chance to respond

Severing communication creates bad blood. Let them ask questions if they have any, and answer those questions in a straightforward, concise manner. Discuss proactively, moving forward – not backward.

Keep emotion out of the situation

You may have developed a friendship with the person, and the termination creates mixed feelings. Convey that the decision is business related and doesn't have to affect the friendship unless the other person chooses to do so. If they do, respect the decision.

Deal with the facts

Avoid going into too much detail, laying blame, or criticizing. Don't drag out the situation by going back over the past if your mind is made up. Move the situation gently forward.

Highlight the positives

There may be a turnaround issue or too many missed deadlines but make an effort to point out something positive, such as great design. Use the negative as suggestions for improvement rather than targeting them solely as faults.

Wish the person good luck

It's important to show no ill will towards the individual. The relationship simply didn't work out for business reasons. Always try to end the discussions on a positive note and part ways as friends.

Ending a relationship can be a difficult thing to do, but if you follow these steps you are likely to have a much better time of it.

> *Take Away Message:*
>
> ***If you cannot troubleshoot a difficult relationship, then it may be necessary to end it. Be straightforward and kind when terminating people, and always show good will and sympathy towards them.***

A Complete Team

Creating a team is one of the biggest steps towards creating a thriving freelance business. As you build your team, your business will become more and more able to expand, and you will have more and more flexibility.

A distributed team is a perfect solution to many of the problems freelancers face on a regular basis. You can begin creating your team with very little money, and you can scale that team and your business to very large sizes.

You can start creating your team with as little as $100 to pay a basic virtual assistant to accomplish some repetitive tasks where your time is more valuable. There's basically no hurdle to jump in order to begin outsourcing, cross-sourcing, and partnering.

Besides the low entry barrier, the great part about creating a distributed freelance team is that you can scale the system to as large as your imagination will let you. We have seen businesses started by a single freelancer evolve into 10 or 20 person teams spread around the globe.

Even if you want to keep your business small, building a team will add redundancy in case of emergencies and allow you to have more flexibility in the work you choose to focus on.

Building a team will allow you to take your freelance business to its full potential.

> ***Take-away Message:***
>
> ***By using different types of people in outsourcing, cross-sourcing, or partnership relationships you can build a team for your business that will help you overcome many of the typical limitations of freelancing. You can start your team with little money, it will be scalable to almost any size, and you can work with people distributed all around the world.***

Resources for Creating Your Team

Throughout this section, we've given you a lot of advice and tips for finding and placing the right people in your team. We talked about why you should build a team, the benefits of a distributed team, how to communicate most effectively when managing projects, how to hire different people for your team, and how to terminate people who aren't pulling their weight. You should have a pretty good idea of what to do.

In this chapter, we have collected a number of the best resources that can help you implement these concepts in your business.

Here are some of our top recommendations:

oDesk http://www.odesk.com/w
This site can be a complete virtual office for your business. You can post jobs and use oDesk to manage and pay the people you've hired. There's also a rating system to determine whether or not an individual has performed well in the past.

Elance http://www.elance.com
Here, you can also post jobs where others can bid on them. Candidate profiles and a rating system are also available. In addition, you can contact individuals directly and ask for proposals.

FreelanceSwitch Job Boards http://jobs.freelanceswitch.com
The job boards on FreelanceSwitch offer another great way to find other freelancers for your team. You can post classifieds on the board for free, and others can view and respond if they feel they're qualified and interested.

IVAA (International Virtual Assistants Association) http://ivaa.org
The IVAA is a non-profit organization for virtual assistants. You can browse through their membership rolls and find a virtual assistant that adheres to their quality standards.

Get Friday http://getfriday.com
This is an outsourcing firm where you can directly hire their members to do your bidding. They have assistants available 24/7 and a variety of pricing options to fit any freelancer's needs.

Other Useful Resources:

http://www.krop.com
http://www.sologig.com
http://www.noagenciesplease.com
http://www.programmermeetdesigner.com
http://www.authenticjobs.com
http://www.guru.com
http://www.craigslist.org
http://www.gofreelance.com
http://www.virtualassistants.com
http://www.virtualassistantnetworking.com
http://www.vanetworking.com/RFP
http://www.virtualassistant.org
http://www.assistu.com
http://www.outsourcing.com
http://www.outsourcing.org
http://www.kayasystems.com
http://www.callruby.com
http://longerdays.com
http://www.asksunday.com

Section Four

Revenue-Generating Assets

Create products and businesses that destroy the time=money relationship and offer enormous potential for income

Benefits of Products and Assets

Freelancers tend to focus heavily on building their client base, and with good reason: they want to have customers, make a name for themselves, and get a reputation that helps drive consumers to their business.

There are other options beyond client work that will create revenue, though, and exploring these options can transform your business. Instead of focusing solely on client work, you can create revenue-generating assets that cost little or nothing to create and that help you earn extra money (or even a full income) for years.

What is a revenue-generating asset?

Very simply, a revenue-generating asset is an item your business owns that generates income. Typically, this asset doesn't require very much or even any of your involvement in order to be profitable.

These assets should bring in revenue on a regular basis. In some cases, the revenue will be entirely passive, with no work from you after its initial creation. In other cases, you may need to put in a little bit of work every so often, but the amount of work required will not be equal to the time you put in. In other words, time will no longer equal money.

Here's a look at the typical time-is-money scenario:

The previous example shows the relationship between time and money that applies to most freelance work. If you were paying close attention earlier, you'll see that this is similar to the diagram in the section about teams and represents an unleveraged income. Using teams can change this equation, and so can building assets.

Here's a diagram of how a revenue-generating asset works:

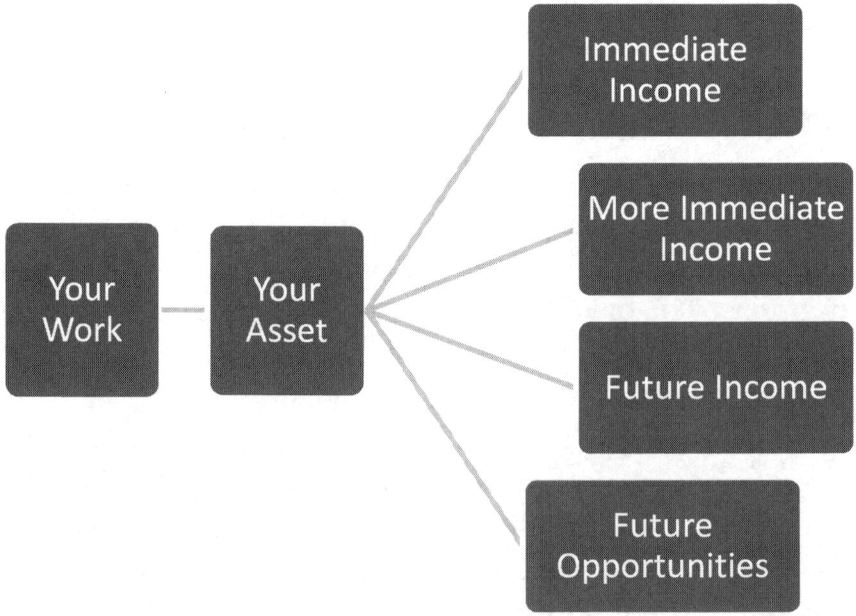

As you can see, this represents another type of relationship that uses leverage; only with assets you are leveraging your work instead of your time. You work once, and then you can benefit from that effort many times over.

Individual assets vary greatly in the amount of income they generate. You may bring in a little from asset A this month, a bit more from asset B, and then the most from asset C. The next month may be entirely different. Having smaller assets, however, can actually be beneficial. Each individual asset does not require much work, and having a more diversified income will provide stability in your business.

Assets, no matter how large they are, have a lot of value to you and your business, and they can usually be sold if you no longer want to manage them.

Some revenue-generating assets you could create include:

- eBooks
- Blogs or websites
- SaaS applications
- Audio files
- T-shirts or other apparel
- Theme templates
- Stock designs
- Photographs
- Membership sites
- Automated courses

…and these are just a handful of ideas. Anything that you can build now and sell multiple times in the future is a potentially great option.

There are many different ways to actually create an asset, too. You could opt to work on it yourself, outsource the development, or partner in a joint-venture agreement. Building a valuable asset doesn't mean you have to do all of the work yourself.

Why are they useful for freelancers?

For freelancers, these assets are useful because they augment and stabilize typical client income. You can continue to work your client projects – your bread and butter – while growing your business' assets.

Putting revenue-generating assets to work for your business has additional advantages beyond the immediate monetary potential. These assets can work as marketing tools as well, spreading your brand, credibility, and reputation to help you bring in new clients and customers.

Creating revenue-generating assets that let you work once and sell many times is a core element to creating a business with unlimited potential. Think about what could happen if you had some additional revenue streams:

- Reduce the risk of work overload and freelancer burnout without stressing over money
- Reduce the number of client projects you take on while still earning income

- Build up a cash bank to have a nest egg for your business in case of emergencies
- Continue to work the hours you do and receive additional income you didn't have before
- Take a break or vacation, fully paid, thanks to the revenue-generating assets you've created

Revenue-generating assets help freelancers work less while still earning a comfortable living. These assets can heighten the joy of your projects, ease your workload, free your time, and help you meet your income needs.

Freelancers already know how to create a valuable asset. You just need to do the same work you do for your other clients – except you're working on your own project.

> *Take-away Message:*
>
> ***Clients are the major source of income for almost every freelancer; but with client projects, time equals money. Revenue-generating assets break the time-equals-money ratio, allowing you to work once and earn income for a long period of time.***

Asset Examples and Ideas

Depending on the type of work you like doing, there are many types of assets you can create. Almost any skill you use when working on your client projects can be turned around and used to create your own assets.

Here's a jump-start list of ideas for products you could create:

Blogs and Websites

A website is almost a necessity for all freelancers, and it's also an extremely valuable asset. Blogs and websites are great to have for any type of freelancer, and they are valuable in more ways than one.

Pros

A website, or a blog, has an extremely valuable resale potential and is easily transferrable if you no longer want to manage it. It can serve as a launch point for other products, provide a business gateway to other services, and can make money by selling advertisements or subscriptions.

Cons

Websites can be difficult to maintain continually, and they need to be nursed for a while before they develop a solid reader base.

It can be challenging to find a topic that will draw enough readers while still being specific enough to be useful. A clean and user-friendly design is also a necessity if you're building your website as an asset.

If you decide that you want to build your website as an asset, you need to write or produce valuable information, build a reader base or community, and then use your site to sell ads, subscriptions, or other products. A quick search on the internet will toss up thousands of other eBooks and resources on how to build your website as an asset.

"One of my wife Cyan's big dreams has always been to travel the world, and in particular to live in different parts of the world… I'd been tossing an idea around about a microstock marketplace for Flash, and the prospect of running a website where no-one would ever really need to phone us or demand last minute revisions to a brochure, sounded pretty good. So we set about building Flash-Den."

Collis Ta'eed, FreelanceSwitch and Envato

Informational Products

Info products, such as eBooks or online courses, are an extremely valuable asset, especially if you're a specialist, expert, or happen to have some sort of valuable knowledge that others seek.

Pros

The number of sales per informational product is limited only by its perceived value in the market. Once the product is created, you do not need to pay for a whole bunch of manufacturing costs that drive profits down. You can simply replicate the product as necessary.

In addition, the quality content that you produce in your product will be valuable to both you and your customers. Your customers will gain the information they seek, and you will gain references from those customers as well as the credibility involved by having created it.

Cons

Informational products have garnered a bad reputation from mass-production and poor-quality content. It's necessary to create quality content and make sure that your potential customers know the value of your product.

In addition, these products take a lot of effort on your part before they are ready to be sold to the masses. While they may provide a lot of income in the long-run, there is a significant, up-front time cost.

To create an informational product as an asset for your business you must first decide on its topic and method of delivery (eBook, course, video, audio book, etc). After you've chosen your specific product, you'll need to take into consideration whether or not you will sell the information as a one-time purchase or as a subscription. Lastly, you need to create a marketing plan that will actually sell enough of the product to make the whole effort profitable – it's easiest when you have a sales platform like a website or a blog.

Stock Photos, Designs, and Theme Templates

Designers and photographers have a great opportunity to create assets out of their photographs, designs, and themes that they are already accustomed to producing.

Pros

A major advantage to creating assets from photographs, designs, and themes is that you do not need your own website to sell them. There are numerous other sites that gather up these items and sell them to the public. In addition, creating one of these assets is something you may already be doing for clients, so they're easy to produce.

Cons

If you use a website other than your own to sell your stuff, there may be significant cuts taken from the total sale of the item. It's important to find a marketplace that will show your item to the biggest audience with the lowest cost to you. It's also difficult to guarantee that your items are unique and valuable – even then, you can't prevent copycats who will reduce the value of your work.

To get started: create your designs, photos, brushes, theme templates, and more, making sure they're original and valuable to the marketplace. Then you can sign up on various sites, such as iStockPhoto.com, FlashDen.com, ThemeForrest.com, and start earning some passive income.

Software, Web Applications, and Plugins

Programmers and coders can build lucrative assets by putting their skills to work on their own projects. Creating software, web applications, and plugins (for everything) are tasks that you are already doing for your clients, so the transition from client work to asset building can be seamless.

Pros

Creating plugins and scripts can be smaller projects that are easy to complete and easy to sell on your own website or a marketplace. Creating software or a web application can develop into an entire business on its own, earning enormous revenue.

Cons

Unless it's a small plugin or script, the time investment for building this type of asset can be high. A lot of marketing is required to make software or web applications successful. Don't forget to make sure the market wants or needs the item you're creating.

If you're looking to work on a plugin or script, you can find ideas by looking through the existing market and trying to find a gap or a need. Once you've developed your item, make a website for the software and sell it both via your website and via other marketplaces.

If you're working on a larger project, like a web application or software package, invest plenty of time in identifying the exact need of your target market before developing your product. Once you've ascertained the need, you can create a site for your product and begin selling it as soon as it is complete.

Physical Products and Merchandise

All types of freelancers can create physical products and merchandise. You can create things as simple as a t-shirt or as complicated as custom-manufactured product.

Pros

If you want to create something simple, you can start by creating a specialty-branded item, like a t-shirt, hat, or a kit. These are easy to create, and there are lots of services available where you can upload your designs and sell your products.

Cons

The profit margin on physical items may be smaller than with digital or information items, as there is a cost for creating products. Holding and maintaining a stock for these items may also be difficult, especially if your items are large or require shipment.

To get started, find a good supplier that gives you a lot of different product options with the least management time and cost involved. Then, decide on what products you think would sell best and create the designs. Finally, market, market, market.

Take-Away Message:

Even if your idea is already out there, you can put a different spin or a unique angle to it and create a meaningful, lasting asset for your business.

No matter what kind of freelancer you are, there are always different assets that can compliment your particular skills and knowledge set. Each type of asset has its own benefits and challenges. Evaluate for yourself and your business which assets would be right for you.

The Right Asset For Your Business

It may seem very obvious to you which revenue-generating asset you should focus on creating for your business. For example, a designer might instantly think of designing the best theme template ever, a writer might immediately leap into building a copywriting course, and a programmer might decide to start on a fantastic application.

Even if that's the case, you should still think about your other options. Sometimes what is very obvious to us may not be the best project to pursue – and other times, the obvious ideas are almost too good to ignore. It pays to consider alternatives.

The general idea of building and maintaining an asset is that it will benefit your business both now and in the future, so choose ideas that are genuinely useful and have the potential to retain that usefulness over time. Be selective and analytical. Opt for assets that have the best potential to achieve the goals you want for you and your business

There are numerous factors involved in choosing the right asset for your particular skill set and business. Investing a little time into planning for your asset or product will go a long way towards its eventual success.

Examine Your Goals, Time, and Money

The amount of available time, money, and expertise you have directly influence what sort of project you should pursue.

Some projects can be too ambitious, end up taking a long time to develop, and then don't even provide the best returns. It's important to determine what type of potential income you may achieve from various projects, from basic to complex.

For example, a template banner may take only a few hours to create, and it could sell itself 100 times. That's a better investment than a complex theme that takes six months to create and sells itself only 25 times.

Big projects need big resources, so find projects that minimize your need to inject time and money while providing optimal returns.

> "Selling stock on the side can provide an extra steady income stream that you can rely on. Whether it's paying a few of your bills, or saving up for your holiday fund. A figure like $200 monthly probably isn't going to change your life, but it does pay for my internet, mobile phone, and moleskine notebooks, and hey that's pretty neat!"
>
> *Collis Ta'eed, FreelanceSwitch and Envato*

How Much Do You Want To Earn?

Knowing how much income you'd like to achieve from a potential asset is an important step to take before you begin to invest resources.

For example, if you decide you want to earn $1,000/mo from your project, selling stock photography may not be the best approach because of the time it will require to reach that level. It may be a better idea to write a book on how to create the best images for stock photography and sell those instead.

Another example is investing your resources into building a membership site only to realize that subscriptions aren't going to achieve your financial goals in the time you desire.

Sometimes, we tend to overestimate how much we can earn from our brilliant ideas. For example, we may create that membership site hoping to earn $97 per sign-up, but the reality may be that signups at that price are too few to sustain the site. It may be necessary to reduce the price and lower overall income expectations.

What Do You Want to Promote?

It is often tempting to build and promote a particular product because it's popular at the time, but that isn't always the right choice. You should ideally select a project that will positively impact other areas of your business and potentially even increase other revenues.

For example, it doesn't make much sense for a copywriter to offer a template design just because it is popular to do so. It's a better idea to create a product that is related to the business and helps boost credibility.

Choose products that help market and promote the other services that you want to sell. Build notoriety and convey expertise. Your assets are there to support and assist your business so that it improves, and being selective about what you promote can make a difference in your long-term success.

Do You Really Want This?

Many people get excited about new ventures, but once they're in the thick of it all, they realize they don't actually like what it takes to maintain the business.

For example, you could decide that you want to build an application and sell it as a web-based service. After launching the service, it becomes necessary to support the customers and the community – which might be something you don’t enjoy. If that’s the case, you will have to either hire someone to perform this function or shut the application down to prevent unhappy customers.

It's always a good idea to create assets that fit well with what you like to do all the time, not just for now. Keep in mind the related tasks you may have to perform and the support you may have to provide on the side.

The ideal plan is to invest your resources in assets that require only the maintenance level you desire and that are in an area of interest that you enjoy.

Match Your Skill Set With a Suitable Asset

There are websites out there that try to sell everything under the sun on a single domain name. We've seen eBooks on personal development being sold alongside others on internet marketing. It makes no sense.

Work on building assets that relate to your business first and foremost, so that you can develop credibility as an expert. Also, consider the fact that the asset you choose could provide a launch point for additional assets that are also related.

For example, if you're a marketer, you could write an eBook on How to Get Your Business Blog Noticed. It's related to your field of expertise, it's unique, and it's in demand. It could also be the launch point for the next two eBooks you've planned: How to Get your Consulting Services Noticed and How to Get your Affiliate Products Noticed.

In that example, your very first asset becomes the beginning of a great series.

Put some thought into the products and assets that you want to build. Try to determine which ones are going to provide the best returns on your investment, and think about whether they help support your overall business goals.

Every asset you build that increases your income and makes your life easier will open even more opportunity for future projects.

You'll be building a business geared for success and a better life for yourself, too.

What Makes You Special?

Competition is everywhere you turn, and differentiating yourself from businesses that provide similar services is important.

Get creative with what you sell. If you're going to sell a course, find an angle to make it different or exciting for subscribers. If you're into design, do something that is rarely seen and make a statement.

Consider specializing and responding to a niche demand that other competitors aren't paying attention to. Also, consider lead-ins for your services. An eBook on how to design RSS buttons, for example, might be a fantastic lead-in to encourage people to hire you for a full website design.

Take-Away Message:

Jumping into the development of the most obvious asset is tempting. It's invigorating to start something new, and your first instinct may turn out to the best match for your business. However, it's important to take the time to think over what you want to create, why you want to create it, and what effect it may have on your business (and you) before you're too far along to turn back.

Choose assets that will give you good long-term results over assets that are popular in the moment. You'll thank yourself for thinking the ideas through from the beginning.

How to Actually Build an Asset

You've read about the value and considerations involved in building an asset, and hopefully you've decided to build an asset for yourself, but where do you start?

Here are some basic steps that will help put you on track for choosing the right asset and beginning its development.

1. **List possible assets – both small and large**
   Grab your pen and paper (or your favorite word processor) and start brainstorming. The crazier the ideas the better, but don't forget to list the obvious ideas too. You can refer to our different types of assets for freelancers if you get stuck, or you can think of ones that weren't even mentioned in this book.

   Include variations of the same asset type and any specific ideas you might have. For example, don't just list eBook, list "eBook on how to take your average freelancing career and turn it into a successful, self-running business."

2. **Choose a few of the best ideas to explore**
   Pick a few of the ideas on your brainstorming list that you particularly like. You might like them because they interest you and you've always dreamed

about something like them. Maybe the ideas you want are the ones that seem like they would be easy to do. Or maybe you want the ones that would be difficult, but would produce amazing results if they came to fruition. It's good to explore a variety of ideas so that you can fully weigh your options.

3. **Examine each idea according to your goals**
   If you don't have specific goals for yourself, take some time to do that now – before continuing to analyze possible assets. With specific goals, you will be able to properly evaluate the different project ideas according to what is most important to you.

   You can do this by breaking up your goals and listing each idea's pros or cons, or you could try to rate each idea on a numeric scale. Either way, devote time to each specific idea, considering how that asset would benefit you and your business.

4. **Examine each idea according to its costs – both time and money**
   Think about how long it would take to create this product. How much time can you devote to developing assets now? Under that constraint, how long would it take for you to build your brand new revenue stream? Are there monetary costs involved? What kind of tasks will be necessary both during and after development for maintaining the asset?

These questions will help you determine whether or not your idea is feasible given your money and time constraints.

5. **Examine each idea according to its potential**
   This step can be tricky, especially if you're not familiar with the market and the competition. Try to determine how successful your ideas will be.

   Is there a market for your idea? How much money will the asset bring in both the long-term and short-term? How much intangible value does the asset have? If your idea may not bring in a lot of money, but will substantially increase your credibility and help you gain bigger and better clients, it may still be worth developing.

6. **Choose your favorite asset (or assets)**
   It's a lot to process, but it's necessary to compile all of the above information and decide on one or more assets you want to develop.

   Remember that you don't need to do all of the feasible assets immediately or at the same time. It's best to choose your number one candidate and begin with that. You can always keep your brainstorming handy for a time when you need inspiration or you've developed an asset fully and want to continue with the others.

7. **Create a development plan**
   It's great to be excited about a new endeavor, but it's important to plan out your next moves so that your dreams actually come true. You don't want to get started working on the design of your new t-shirt only to realize that none of the suppliers you like are able to use that design due to manufacturing constraints.

   Doing your research and planning your specific path to implementation will save you time and frustration. It's also good to create goals with timelines and milestones and to set aside some time each week to work on the implementation of the plan.

Developing Your Assets

If you're planning on creating a revenue-generating asset for your business, there's one crucial point you need to keep in mind at all times: you are your client.

It's too easy for freelancers to put their personal projects aside when client work comes in. They call it 'downtime' work – filler – and they push it off to take on work that brings in short-term income. That could be a big mistake. We all seem to need money these days, but cheating yourself out of projects that you and your business need in the name of fast cash is the wrong way to go.

Passive income sources help stabilize and even increase typical client income. They can reduce the feast or famine cycle, they can improve business revenues, and they can spread credibility and notoriety to draw in new clients.

If you get into the bad habit of setting aside your own projects when clients come calling, you may never see these projects through to completion. It's voluntarily opting out on making your life better.

What's even worse is when personal projects never get started. They stay just a dream forever, because it's too easy to tell ourselves, "Someday..." and then someday never comes. All you have is today (and the tomorrow that you can shape and influence by making smart choices right now).

The smartest choice you can make is to understand that you are your most valuable customer and that you should treat yourself as you would any other client. Take your idea for a passive income source and give it a deadline. Set milestones. Plan the progress. Spread it over a few weeks if you need to, but always make sure that the project never stagnates or gets set aside.

Reserve a few hours each week for your project and it will progress smoothly and steadily. You'll have time to work on client projects and short-term goals the rest of the week, and you'll be moving steadily towards your own future goals and dreams as well.

Remember, too, that creating a revenue-generating asset for your business doesn't mean you have to do it alone. Outsource part of the project, collaborate with other people in joint ventures, or hire someone to do the basic work and save you some time. You can add your special touch afterwards.

This book is all about finding ways to improve your business, free up your time, and do what you want to do. You can start right now by beginning a personal project that will bring you both satisfaction and revenue.

About Dreams and Ambition

Most freelancers are ambitions people. They're creatives, dreamers, and visionaries. It almost goes without saying that freelancers have all sorts of great ideas and ambitious projects.

Spontaneous plans, dreams, and ideas are a good thing, and they're crucial to creating a successful small business – but overly ambitious dreams can become a problem if they prevent you from taking care of your business. Small business owners seem to be very susceptible to this, often forgetting about their business because dreaming is fun.

Have a special place where you can write down your dreams, your ambitions, and your ideas. Save the dreams that aren't practical or realistic for sometime in the future. Revisit them from time to time, if you'd like, but set those dreams aside if you can't realize them immediately.
Big dreams can be reached, but they're reached by being productive with the reality you have now. Build on your business and work at making it better. One day, you'll look at your dream file and realize that you're in a position to actually start moving forward on one of those ambitious dreams.

Chasing the Illusion of Perfection

The desire to wow people and have them admire your work is a normal one that you most likely share with many, many people. We all want to receive praise and compliments; and stunning someone into speechless awe is a fantastic reward for a job well done. That reward can also become a problem for freelancers.

It's easy to get caught in the trap of seeking perfection. We want to do a good job, but sometimes we begin to doubt our own abilities and hold off launching products or services because we hear internal whispers that tell us, "This isn't good enough yet. It's not perfect."

The problem with perfection is that it's subjective and, by some definitions, impossible to achieve. Everyone perceives greatness in different ways. What is trash to you may be gold to another and vice versa. No clear-cut definitions guide us, and personal definitions of 'perfect' are different from person to person.

Work towards the goal of creating great products. Be ambitious, certainly, but be realistic as well. If your revenue-generating asset offers customers a useful solution, then it's going to be a success.

Learn to recognize when you've done a good job and when to stop. Be respectful of yourself, and give yourself permission to be human – not perfect. Perfection is just a myth.

Tips to Nip Perfectionist Tendencies in the Bud

If you're a perfectionist, it can be tough to learn how to expect less from yourself. It can be done, though, with a little effort and some consistent self-monitoring.

Here are tips that can help:

- Think about whether you would hold others to the same standards that you're holding yourself.
- Ask someone to look over what you've done, and see if they would be satisfied with what you've created.
- If you start to feel overwhelmed by a project, get some distance and rethink your situation.
- Ask yourself to rate the importance of launching a "perfect" product on a scale of one to ten. Will people even notice the tiniest details you've been focusing on? Or will you have to point out what you've done?
- Is what you're working on going to have a substantial impact on the product? Does it really matter?
- Examine your perceptions and the realities. Imagine all the possible outcomes if you launched now, from best to absolute worst. Then ask yourself how you'd handle those worst-case scenarios, and pretend you had to deal with them.

Putting your work out for sale can be a nerve-wracking experience, but thankfully, feeling nervous about a product launch is usually temporary. Once the first week or two passes, you'll most likely realize that you were stressing over nothing and that the situation was far less monumental than you believed it to be.

Take-away Message:

Choosing the right asset to develop isn't easy. Consider each idea to its fullest potential, and you'll be able to choose which one is best for you and your business. Once you've decided on an asset, create a plan for developing it to fruition.

Set deadlines, milestones, and schedules that help your project progress. Work with others, and leverage resources to create passive income sources that will give even more free time (and money) later on. Remember: you are your most valuable client, and working on your goals will ultimately get you to where you want to be.

Resources for Creating and Selling Your Products

There are a ton of online resources for creating and marketing all sorts of assets. Depending on what you're looking to create, there may be one or one thousand websites that can help you in the process. We've scoured the web for some of the best tools, so make sure you check out the list below before getting started.

Here are our recommendations:

Zazzle http://www.zazzle.com
You can use this site to create various types of merchandise for your business. They have many different products, and you can sell the things you create directly on your site. When you sell your products, Zazzle fulfills all of the orders, so you do not need to maintain any inventory.

Lulu http://www.lulu.com
This site is a publishing service where you can put your informational product (book, cookbook, photo album, cds…) into production. They have low quantity requirements and lots of options that will help you customize your product how you see fit.

iStockphoto http://www.istockphoto.com
Not only is this site a great place to buy stock media, it's a great place to sell your photography, illustrations, and

video as well. You will need to apply to the site to become a contributor, and your income will depend on the popularity of your contributions.

Theme Forest http://www.themeforest.net
Envato's theme marketplace is a great place to sell your website themes for any CMS. You'll need to sell the themes you submit exclusively through the marketplace, and you'll receive 25% - 50% of the item's selling price depending on how well your item sells.

Other Places to Sell Your Stuff:

http://www.cafepress.com
http://www.clickbank.com
http://www.cdbaby.net
http://www.e-junkie.com
http://www.1shoppingcart.com
http://www.foxycart.com
http://flashden.net
http://audiojungle.net
http://videohive.net
http://www.scripts.com
http://www.hotscripts.com
http://www.promopeddler.com
http://www.empirepromos.com

Section Five

Combine Strategies for Unlimited Potential

How to combine all of your tools and strategies to create a business with unlimited potential

A Unified Combination

The most efficient and prosperous businesses are the ones that combine all of the various strategies into a single, unified whole. Many elements of a successful freelance business simply don't work well alone. For the best results, they need to be used in coordination with other tools.

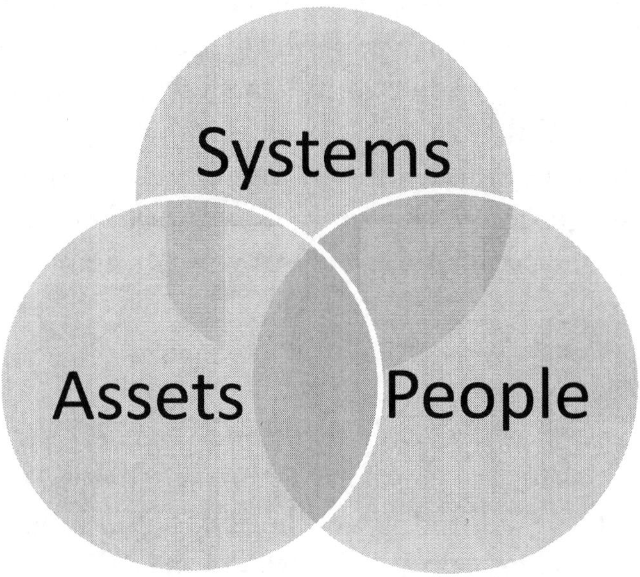

Collaboration is the perfect example of an area that works best with the support of another system. You can collaborate without the need for anything else, but to truly reap the benefits of a collaborative team, it is necessary to use some sort of project management application that allows the sharing of information, concepts, and ideas.

When you combine both the system and the team, you're left with an efficient business that can tackle many more projects with much better results.

This same concept applies to other areas of business, too. Using an accounting system along with a paid bookkeeper, for example, is another combination that works better than either of the parts alone.

As a third example, some very profitable assets require complex systems and outsourcing in order to be worthwhile. A website that relies on the content-advertiser business model can be incredibly profitable, but it can also be incredibly difficult and time consuming to manage. If you built the site onto a content management system, and hired a manager to coordinate writers and collect payment from advertisers, you'd be left with a very profitable website that practically runs itself. That is the power of properly combining systems, software, and people.

Some areas of business only need one strategy. But there are many areas of your business where you'll need to use a combination to pull it all together, creating a support net that makes sure you accomplish what you desire. You may need two or three combined strategies for the most efficient and best results.

Systems, Outsourcing, and DIY: Which and When?

When you sit back and think of all the big areas of your business, like marketing, production, accounting and customer service, it can all be a little overwhelming trying to decide what to do where and how to create the best business ever.

Remember, though, that every area of business has its own set of smaller areas. Break it down into manageable bits, especially when you're starting out. Accounting, the larger area, includes smaller areas like invoicing, collections, bookkeeping, budgeting, etc. Each of these areas can be worked on individually and improved to reach better efficiency that increases the efficiency of the whole business.

A business is a huge system, with each tiny task influencing the success of the whole.

When trying to determine what needs a system, what should be outsourced, and what should be done by you, carefully examine each task and its related areas of your business. Ask yourself a few questions and contemplate the answers:

Is this task time-consuming?

Time-consuming tasks reduce your ability to accept paying work that brings in money. They're energy drainers that often cost your business more than a little in lost work hours.

Very often, someone else can perform the task, which frees up time to work on client projects and brings in new customers, allowing you to earn more revenues and achieve better profits overall.

Does this task require specialized skills?

If you're working on a task that isn't in your usual skill set, you could be making costly mistakes, taking too long to complete the task, or creating frustration in yourself because you're not sure of what to do. This is a case of freelancers wearing hats they don't have to.

Tasks that fall outside your specialty or usual skill set are ones that could usually be performed and completed by someone else with more relevant and pertinent skills.

Is this a task I enjoy working on?

There is no rulebook that says freelancers have to perform tasks they don't like. If you hate something, don't do it. Find someone else who does enjoy that type of work and let them do it.

You'll find yourself less stressed, less frustrated, and happier, which are three feelings that just can't be beat.

What could I do if I didn't have this task?

Think about what you would do if you suddenly didn't have to work on this task. Where would you focus? Would you work on getting better paying jobs, progressing on personal projects, or resting more and spending time with your family?

Be selfish with your personal time. If you know there are personal projects that you could complete to make your life better or that there are client projects you would take on to have better income or satisfaction, then make those a priority.

Does this task require my personal creativity?

Some things you do regularly will require your personal attention and creativity. In many of those cases, it's best to do the work on your own and let your passion show through.

Be careful, though, because some tasks are misleading and only make you *think* that they require your attention, when they actually don't require any personal touch at all. If you have the feeling that a certain task may fall into that category, it's probably best to investigate other possibilities for having it completed.

Very few business-related tasks require your personal creativity, insight, or brainpower to complete. Even those tasks that seemingly depend solely on you are often ones that someone can do just as well, only differently.

With clear instructions, could anyone do this task?

Freelancers often get caught in the cycle of thinking no one can do what they do. Their email inbox is special, no one would understand his or her method of accounting, and who could possibly know exactly how to do X, Y, or Z task?!

Well, if you can write down a clear set of step by step instructions for the task, then you can give that to anyone to handle. Hoarding tasks by thinking we're the only person who can do them is a costly, energy-sapping mistake.

Does this task depend on other people?

Knowing which tasks don't depend on anyone in particular, which tasks require two or more people involved, and which tasks need a complete team effort is important.

This helps you choose which strategies you'll need to implement in order to pull it all together as a success. Tasks that need no one particular person working on them can usually be outsourced immediately to free up time.

How much time would I gain if someone else did this task?

Financial advisors say that it's often best to put all our focus on chipping down the biggest debts first. In business, the same rule of thumb applies.

If you can shed a task that frees up a great deal of time, go for it. You can use that time more productively on projects that really matter. If all you'll save is a few minutes, focus on another task to shed instead.

Do I really need to do this task?

Freelancers often end up collecting all sorts of work for themselves that doesn't need to be done. Being busy doesn't equal being productive. Even more, collecting tasks and work to do makes people feel guilty or resentful that they can't get to the work that they'd really like to do.

Get rid of the fluff and focus on what really matters. Ask yourself if the task is necessary and crucial to operations. If it isn't, then eliminate it and enjoy immediate free time.

Is there a software system that can handle this?

So many people use manual methods or outdated ways to perform tasks, such as using an Excel spreadsheet for bookkeeping.

Software developers often have automated solutions that do a better, faster job at certain tasks (like QuickBooks for accounting), which help free up time and increase accuracy.

Do I feel strongly about this task and need to perform it myself?

There are some tasks in business that we feel strongly about doing ourselves. Some people definitely want to manage their own email for privacy reasons. Others hold tight to accounting, project management, or marketing.

If you love something and enjoy doing it, then hang onto that. Just make sure that you're hanging onto work that you like and want to do – and that you're not holding on just because you can't let go.

Separating Tasks into Groups

When you really sit down and think about everything you do in a day, you may find that there are many tasks in your business that aren't necessary to your satisfaction, happiness, or personal fulfillment. These are prime tasks to shed from your workload.

You might discover some tasks can be done away with completely. They are unnecessary weight, and your business will still operate just fine without them. It's amazing how much additional work we create for ourselves that we really don't need to do.

You may also realize that there are many tasks that you do that you aren't particularly qualified to do in the first place. It's a mistake to continue struggling with them, as the risk of frustration, stress, and error is high. For example, some people admit having poor math skills. Bookkeeping would not be the best work for them to perform.

Run down the list of tasks and work that you perform in your business. Try to group tasks into three lists: potential outsource, potential application, and do myself. You're on your way to a good start.

Take a look at the potential outsource list you've created. If anything on that list doesn't involve more than one person, you can outsource it safely. Create a list of step-by-step instructions, make sure they're concise, and send it off!

If there are tasks that do require the involvement of more than one person, you know that you should set up a good collaboration system and find reliable partners. This is one case where multiple strategies could work together.

Check the potential application list next. Research some good applications that respond to the need of the task as closely as possible. Then decide whether the data entry or management can be outsourced, too. This is another case of multiple strategies working together.

You may decide that the automation of a task doesn't really reduce the time it takes for its completion; it's smarter to keep the data entry as a task you perform. Just make sure the time you invest doesn't cost your business too much.

Figure out if any areas on the DIY (do-it-yourself) list could benefit from a good system or a more efficient process. Write down the steps you take to perform each task. Then take another look at the task – now that you've written down the steps and created instructions, do you still feel you need to perform the task yourself? If not, outsource.

Always strive to reduce the amount of time and energy that goes into your business until it becomes an efficient, streamlined machine.

By putting thought into what you do and investing enough time to examine your operations, you may realize that you can shed a great deal of work that you do for your business to create a freelance business that works for you.

> ***Take-away Message:***
>
> ***The best businesses use teams, systems, and assets together to create one beautiful business that runs smoothly. Take the time to examine everything you do in your business, and combine the various tools and strategies to handle that work in the best way possible.***

How to Be Selfish the Right Way

Taking care of yourself and your business is important. It's terribly easy to get caught up in the cycle of working for clients, bringing in money, getting new work, bringing in more money… and besides, you may really need that money.

That means personal projects get pushed aside. That's also a common mistake.

It's important to be selfish with your time and energy. Continually spending it on areas that don't improve your business holds you back from a better life. You'll always be stuck where you are, and your business won't be able to do everything it can for you.

For example, you may have plans to design a blog theme that people buy, creating passive income. So you work on this project in your spare time, and it advances. Slowly.

Each time a client comes with work for you, you set aside your personal project for the immediate income potential. When the client work is completed, you may feel too tired to pick up your project again, so you let a few days go by. Maybe you lost your inspiration. Maybe you just have too many clients to work on the design at all.

You're stuck. You wanted to create that passive income to get your business working harder for you so that you could work less, but other work just keeps coming and there's never any time.

Here's another example: You want to integrate a good step-by-step system to prepare for collaboration and set up a good process with the right application. But paying clients come first, so you tend to their needs. Then demand increases and you decide to start collaborating so you can take on more projects and earn more revenues.

But your system isn't ready, the process is difficult and you end up deciding your business isn't ready – which means you're stuck staying small when you were ready to grow.

Be selfish with your time. You are your own client and you deserve just as much attention you're your projects as you would give anyone else. Invest in your personal needs so that you can achieve the goals you want.

One good way to make sure that you continue to progress on your personal projects is to treat them as you would any other work for a customer. Set up deadlines and milestones. Schedule your time. Commit yourself, and reserve an hour each day or a few hours per week for your own projects so that they progress towards completion.

Hold yourself accountable, too. Would you continually miss a client's deadline and present the person with excuses? Of course not! So have that same integrity towards yourself. Don't present yourself with excuses, meet the obligations you have to reach your dreams, and dedicate some of your time to fulfill your goals.

It's crucial. Take care of yourself and your business above all, so that you can find that freelancing freedom you've dreamed of. Work on personal projects as hard as you would a client project, especially those that improve and better your business or that increase your free time and revenues.

It may be tough to say no when a client comes calling and asks for immediate help. The lure of immediate revenue can be tempting. Stand your ground, though. Maintain your dedication, and see your projects through.

A little time investment now can result in a huge impact down the line – and definitely for the better.

Take-away Message:

When you're a freelancer, it can be easy to fall into a vicious cycle of working so hard that you don't have the time to work on areas that help you work less.

Be selfish with your personal projects. Give them just as much attention as you would a client project, and help them progress towards completion so that you achieve the goals you want.

Your Business: Low-Cost, Flexible, and Fully Scalable

Building a business doesn't require that you go back to the drawing board and scramble to build it up quickly. Too many freelancers make that mistake, slapping on fast, band-aid patches that work for right now. At the first bit of pressure, those makeshift processes crumble.

Building a good, solid business takes time. The beauty of this business model is that it lets you grow in the time that you want to, requires no major financial investment on your part, and is completely scalable to adjust to your needs.

Of course, some practices outlined in this book can be put into place right now, and they'll have an immediate impact on your overall free time, income, and satisfaction.

In general, though, building a business ready and secure for the future involves some thought, analysis, attention, and follow-through. The changes you make and the systems you apply need to be monitored for efficiency. Improvements need to be incremental and tweaked to get the best results.

Your business needs time to grow while you set the foundation. You'll also need time to become habituated with new methods of working. Give them a chance, and give each method a full two weeks to a month of continual practice to ingrain the habit.

It's worth it. Your efforts and conscientious focus will ultimately provide you with more free time to do what you love, more of the work you enjoy, and more customers bringing you the jobs you love.

Time is on your side. Creating processes, applying systems, incorporating applications, and leveraging resources do not need immediate implementation. Build slowly, build carefully, and build well. You'll thank yourself for it.

Your wallet will thank you, too. Building a good freelancing business doesn't require a huge investment and can even be carried out with no financial investment from your pocket at all. You can collaborate with someone else using only your time and skills to create a source of income, or you can take your first client paycheck and use it to hire an outsourcer.

You don't have to work with other people right away either. You can implement systems and good business practices that prepare your business for the future, but there's no need to work with others if you have no interest. You'll be ready if that day should come, that's all.

If you do want to work with others? This business model gives you the potential to grow your business easily and seamlessly. You can scale your business from one person to 1.5 to 2 to 3 and back down again if you wish without a hitch.

Your business model adjusts exactly to your needs, and it's easily adjusted to meet customer demands. This scalability lets you take the time to get everything right and grow slowly over time – implementing improvements and monitoring their effects so you can have a business that works hard for you without you working hard for it.

Take your time. Get it all set up the way you want it. Find the most efficient way of working that fits right for you. Focus on what you want to do, and leverage the resources you have at your fingertips to get the other work done too.

Build the business you've dreamed of: one that provides you with more of what you want and need.

Take-away Message:

Many freelancers are so excited to leap into business that they slap their business model together quickly and consider it done. Building a good business takes time.

Our business model provides the time you need to build that solid business, and it's one that is fully scalable to meet your needs – and give you more of what you want.

Make Your Own Rules

No one likes to be told what to do, ourselves included. That said, thinking over suggestions and giving new methods a decent shot is worth exploring.

Many of our business practices were discovered by trial and error – and they definitely aren't new. They've been covered elsewhere, only never in one central resource.

Why is that? Why are good business practices so scattered far and wide? Why has no one created the Freelancer's Bible so that virtual workers everywhere can succeed?

Well, truthfully, they very well may have. We've read plenty of books that offer sound business models that do work. They just don't work for us. The same will happen with you: some techniques and strategies won't work as well for you as others will – and that's okay.

You and your business are unique. You have unique needs, a unique personality, and a unique way of working. That means you need to know when to do what's right for you, without ignoring suggestions that might help you along the way.

You'll find people with very successful businesses giving good advice on various tactics and strategies. Try them, and give those suggestions your all for at least two weeks. If they don't work for you and they're not a good fit, try something else.

There is no cookie-cutter model out there for businesses. No single rulebook says, "This is the way to do it so that you will always have success." Promising success based on one method only is impossible, considering how much uniqueness goes into each business.

You'll need to try various ways, explore different methods and find ways of working that fit best with you. As long as you continually strive for improvements and always keep an open mind on new ways of working, you'll do just fine.

For example, most business experts suggest making yourself as available as possible to clients. Yet we know some successful business owners who communicate only via email. They do it that way because it works best for them.

Figure out methods that give you the most success for your business with the least amount of effort and time while producing the best results. Test, try, and if you've given it your all and it just isn't working for you, then try something different.

What's important is that you continually explore ways to free your time and have heightened efficiency for your business so that your days become ones you enjoy, not ones you don't want to face. That's all part of the goal: more time, more money and a life you enjoy.

So make improvements to your business, yes. Give everything a fair shot and enough time to work. Don't toss out suggestions you've applied because they don't feel right after only a few days. Habits take two weeks to form (at least), so let that period pass before making a decision.

Give every option a fair chance, too. Embrace new methods and give them your all, even if you have doubts that they'll work for you. You may be surprised that a strategy you were skeptical about truly does have a huge influence on the satisfaction level you feel each day.

The moral? Follow the instructions, follow your heart, and improvise to do what's right for you. You just may discover a better way of working.

Take-away Message:

Many freelancers feel intimidated by expertise and follow instructions to the letter. Later, they become frustrated when they can't get the "recipe" to work.

It's okay to set down the instructions and do what works best for you. There are no rules, and this is your business, so make it what you want it to be and enjoy it.

Success When You Least Expect It

We always hope for success in our endeavors, but very few freelancers believe they'll actually achieve success. As the saying goes, hope for the best and plan for the worst.

That means freelancers (and most business people, in fact) focus on possibilities such as a slow startup, periods of no income and the need for safety nets and backup plans. They plan for the challenges, the obstacles, and the slow periods.

They rarely plan for success.

But sometimes, business takes off in ways that you least expect. You may have had plans to stay small, but suddenly you find yourself swamped with customers clamoring to work with you. Your waiting list grows, you're trying to find time to do everything, demand may be higher than you predicted…

In short, your success happened much sooner than you thought it would.

That's a dangerous time for any business. A business that grows too fast and too soon needs a solid foundation and strong support to weather the crazy period. Preparing for growth – even if you have no plans at all to grow – makes sure that your business (and you) survives this exciting but extremely demanding period.

"Survives?" We can hear the questions now. "Come on. Wow! Success! It must be such an easy life!"

That's what many people are thinking, but ask anyone who experienced a sudden rise to near-fame about how easy success truly is. You may be surprised at the answer. Just look at how many celebrities shoot to stardom – and end up folding under pressure.

A growth spurt is terribly fantastic but also incredibly demanding. Trying to control a business ballooning out of size before your very eyes can be startling. Many freelancers don't know what to do. They try to stop the growth and hold it back. They try to just hang on and hope the craziness stops soon.

It's easy to become drained or even exhausted managing everything going on (and it all tends to happen at once). A solid foundation for your business helps make sure you're more prepared to handle the unexpected.

Most business growth is temporary. It eventually slows and stabilizes, but no one knows when that moment may be. Growth can plateau quickly or continue over a longer period. You need to make sure you can weather the ride.

An efficient operating process, good systems, reliable support partners, and timesaving methods help a great deal. Instead of scrambling to manage the growth, you'll only have to make small adjustments. Even if you don't intend to grow your business and want to keep it small, prepare for the possibility that growth may happen whether you want it to or not.

The efforts you put into practice now will be working hard for you, and you'll be much more able to withstand the stress of success. With the right systems in place, a collaboration plan set up, and your mindset ready to help you and your business, you can ride the wave of success – enjoy the ride.

Take-away Message:

Most freelancers expect a slow growth while the business becomes established. Few expect resounding success, and they often cave under the pressure of a growing business with demanding needs.

Making sure that you have a solid foundation in place now – even if you don't plan to grow your business – can help you weather a sudden rise to glory. It just may happen!

Don't Turn Your Back on Growth

Many freelancers don't want to grow their business. They're quite content on their own and have no particular interest in a bigger venture. They aren't attracted by the idea of working with others or retiring and letting someone else do the work they love.

That's fantastic. Knowing what you want in your life is very important, and there are no rules that say a business has to be small, medium or large. If you're happy with your business as-is, then enjoy it and make it the best it can be to give you what you want and need.

But growth doesn't have to mean expansion. Growth in many businesses doesn't equate to added personnel or added work hours. It could be that for your business growth means more flexibility, better cash reserves, and a more stable long-term outlook.

How you choose to apply the strategies in this book are up to you – and it doesn't always need to be expansion.

It's also a good idea to keep your options open for the possibility of expansion in the future.

Today, you may want a small business that is fully self-reliant. Tomorrow, your situation may change. Growth potential provides options; future opportunities may not be attractive now but might one day be exactly what you want.

For example, what if in five years you decide that you'd like to branch out into new areas of business? What if you'd like to move away from your current business and build a new one? What if you decide that you'd like to travel for a year and have your business provide you with income? What if an injury prevents you from working and you need to find ways to maintain your income stream?

Knowing what you want in life now is very important to your personal satisfaction. Keeping your options open for the future is a very smart idea. Improvement should be constant, and expansion should always be a possibility.

Remember, you may not want what you have right now for the rest of your life. Tomorrow, next month or next year, you may want something very different.

Always keep your future options open, and set up your business so that if you do choose to travel a different life path later on, your business will be prepared to handle the adjustment easily.

You may never change path at all, and that's fine. But if one day you decide to change your life, your business should be ready to help you get to where you want to be, and you'll have an easier time building a life you love.

"I wanted to be an editor or a journalist, I wasn't really interested in being an entrepreneur, but I soon found I had to become an entrepreneur in order to keep my magazine going."

Richard Branson, Virgin Group Ltd.

Take-away Message:

Many freelancers enjoy owning a small business and have no plans at all for expansion. This doesn't mean turning your back on growth and improvement, though. It's also a good idea to leave the door open for becoming a bigger business. Always plan for unexpected life changes, and remember that you might have different goals and preferences in the future.

Optimize your business as much as possible now to keep your options open later.

Now it's Your Turn

You've read the book, you've got the knowledge, and you've got the tools – now it's time to put them into practice. This is an opportunity for you to change your business, and potentially to change your life.

Many freelancers have made the transition from having a work-at-home job to owning a freelance business, and some of them have done it spectacularly. Some of the resources you've seen in this book were started by freelancers who, just like you, wanted something more from their business. Now many of them manage distributed teams with dozens of people, run their businesses on an entirely systematized foundation, and are successful beyond belief. You can get there too.

Building a business can be hard work, and don't listen to anyone who tells you otherwise, but the work is almost always worth the effort. The freedom and opportunities that you can have as a freelance business owner are truly unbelievable and much closer than you might think.

Good luck – we wish you the best.

Mason, James, and the entire FreelanceFolder.com team

Further Reading

A lot of the information in this book was inspired by books and authors who came before us. In this section you'll find a few resources that extend or comment on the information in this book, and also some things that are completely unrelated but extremely valuable in other ways.

Books

The E-Myth by Michael Gerber
The Four-Hour Work Week by Tim Ferris
Made To Stick by Chip & Dan Heath

Websites

FreelanceFolder.com
FreelanceSwitch.com
MenWithPens.ca
FreelanceWritingGigs.com
WebWorkerDaily.com
Copyblogger.com
FuelYourCreativity.com
JustCreativeDesign.com
Problogger.com
DesignM.ag
TheDesignCubicle.com
SmashingMagazine.com
OutlawDesignBlog.com
Anti9to5Guide.com

And Many Others…